Man the Messenger

French army wireless telegraphists at work near the front in the
First World War.

Man the Messenger

Edwin Packer

PRIORY PRESS LIMITED

Social History of Science Library

Man the Astronomer *Patrick Moore*
Man the Builder *John Harvey*
Man the Explorer *G R Crone*
Man the Farmer *Robert Trow-Smith*
Man the Navigator *E W Anderson*
Man and the Wheel *D S Benson*
Man the Industrialist *Peter Hobday*
Man the Toolmaker *Michael Grey*
Man and Measurement *Keith Ellis*
Man and Money *Keith Ellis*
Man the Shipbuilder *Maurice Griffiths*
Man the Homemaker *D C Money*
Man the Messenger *Edwin Packer*
Man and the Atom *J K Thomson*
Man the Timekeeper *Brian Hellyer*
Man the Warrior *D C Money*
Man the Steelmaker *W K V Gale*
Man the Aviator *E W Anderson*

SBN 85078 153 1
Copyright © 1974 by Edwin Packer
First published in 1974 by
Priory Press Ltd
101 Grays Inn Rd, London WC1
Text set in Baskerville
and printed in Great Britain by
Page Bros (Norwich) Ltd, Norwich

Contents

1 The First Messages — 9
2 Writing From a Distance — 19
3 The Early Messengers — 25
4 The English Revival — 35
5 The Modern Post Office — 43
6 The Uses of Printing — 53
7 The Growth of the Press — 63
8 Telegraph and Telephone — 75
9 Sending Messages Through the Air — 91
10 Records, Cinema, Television — 101
11 Today and Tomorrow — 116
Date Chart — 121
Picture Credits — 124
Glossary — 125
For Further Reading — 127
Index — 128

List of Illustrations

	on page
French army wireless telegraphists	frontispiece
Laying a submarine telephone cable	8
An African signalling drum	11
Newsboys with horns	12
A French Guards drummer, 1635	13
The Scots Greys at Waterloo	14
Lighting the Armada beacons	15
The Pharos of Alexandria	16
The Roman lighthouse at Dover	16
Eddystone lighthouse	17
A sheepdog at work	19
"England Expects . . ."	21
Signalling by flag in 1917	22
Balloons leaving besieged Paris, 1871	23
A Phoenician inscription	25
Pheidippides arrives in Sparta	26
Paul Revere's midnight ride	27
A Babylonian carving	28
A Greek runner	29
Mercury, messenger of the gods	30
Cuneiform text	31
A letter written on papyrus	32
A Roman signalling post	33
A medieval messenger	34
A medieval illustrated manuscript	34
A Stuart foot postman	36
Seventeenth century bookbinding	37
A writing master's copy sheet, 1600	38
The first London to Bath mail coach	39
Stuck in a drift of snow	41
The first post box	43
The Penny Black	44
A London postman	44
HM Packet *Granville* is attacked	45
The record-breaking *Great Western*	46
Carriages on the Liverpool and Manchester railway	47
The Post Office in 1844	48
The first scheduled London to Paris flight	49
The crash of the Hindenburg	51
A page from a Saxon manuscript	52
Copying a manuscript	54
Caxton is presented to Edward IV	55
A sixteenth century printing press	56

The first Bible printed in English   57
A pamphlet of 1613   58
Printing in the seventeenth century   61
An eighteenth century political cartoon   64
A merchant's card   65
The reforming John Wilkes   66
Eighteenth century printing   67
Victorian newspaper advertisements   68–9
The *Daily Telegraph*'s printing machine, 1860   71
Selling newspapers   73
The poster announcing the news of Trafalgar in London   74
Cooke's and Wheatstone's two-needle telegraph   76
Wheatstone's telegraph, 1840   77
Samuel Finley Breese Morse   78
Putting up the telegraph wire   79
The launching of the *Faraday*   81
The telegraph office in the City of London, 1871   83
The assassination of President Lincoln   84
Alexander Graham Bell   86
Bell's first telephone   87
Bell's newspaper advertisement   88
Bell makes the first call from New York to Chicago   90
Ethel le Neve dressed as a boy   92
Marconi with his assistant   93
Marconi's wireless station at Poldhu   94
Flying the kite in Newfoundland   95
SS *Titanic* on her trials   96
The *Titanic*'s last message   97
An early radio broadcast   100
Thomas Edison   102
An 1899 advertisement for a phonograph   103
An Edwardian family admires a new gramophone   104
Edison's electric animated pictures   105
A still from one of the earliest films   106
Hollywood in its early days   107
A Russian still   109
A scene from *The Jazz Singer*   109
Baird and the beginning of television   111
The first men on the moon   114–15
Checking a new satellite   117
A modern Post Office sorting machine   118

The Post Office starts to lay a new submarine telephone cable to Spain from a Cornish beach.

1: The First Messages

We are social animals. For most of our lives we mix with others in groups from choice. We live in a family. At the end of childhood, when we are old enough to leave the family group, we usually go to live with someone of the opposite sex to start a family group of our own. We take part in games with others and we combine with others at work to produce some article or to provide some sort of service for other people.

Man is not unique in being a social animal. Many other species besides man are social in their organization. Yet these other animals have not achieved the same mastery over their environment as man has, a mastery now so great that he can do almost anything he puts his mind to. Mainly this is due to something which is unique, man's instinctive drive to *know*, to find out more and more. No other animal possesses this.

These two characteristics, the urge to combine with others and the urge to know, have been the driving force behind the development of communications. They led man over many thousands of years to create a complex system of speech sounds called language. Later he invented methods of recording these combination of sounds, by using letters and drawings, so that they would not be forgotten and would always be available for reference. Other animals are able to communicate with each other by language, but the number of sounds they use is small.

Because we are social animals we like to tell what we know. Everyone finds it hard to keep a secret. So alongside the growth of social units—families combining to form tribes, tribes combining to form nations —there has been a corresponding growth of communication. Whatever activity man has engaged in throughout history he has found that communication helped him both to do it more successfully and to tell other people how it was done.

As soon as man became vocal he used sound to tell others what he was thinking. Hunters used it 10,000 years ago when tracking animals for food. Creeping up on their prey they kept silent. Then the kill, launched from several sides, was signalled by a sound which carried a special meaning: "Attack!"

Xerxes, the Emperor of Persia who ruled from 486 to 464 B.C., selected men whose voices carried a long way and whose hearing was good to man a string of call-posts across his empire, relaying messages that were shouted from post to post. Over long distances this was quicker than sending a runner or rider with the message, for sound travels at about 745 miles per hour, or about 12 miles a minute.

There were serious disadvantages to this method when there were high winds or sandstorms; but it was fairly efficient, otherwise it would not have remained in use for hundreds of years. Julius Caesar wrote of the call-post system in Gaul: "The news of the rebellion spread quickly through all the provinces of Gaul. Loud calls carried the news from place to place. What happened at sunrise at Genatum was known before sunset at Auvernum, a distance of 160,000 double feet." This distance was about 450 miles.

But the most far-reaching, efficient and weather-resistant of these early methods of communication was the drumbeat. Archaeologists say it is likely that Stone Age tribes used a drum made of animal skin stretched over a piece of hollow tree trunk; and the first Europeans to land in South America and Central

Primitive African broadcasting: this signalling drum of the
Tucano tribe was in use in 1923.

Africa found a system of sending messages by drumbeat which was superior to any signalling system possessed at that time by the white man.

The sounds produced by the drum in the hands of an expert convey the message through the rhythm and strength of the beats. Deep drumbeats can be heard clearly over a distance of six miles, and in valleys (where the sound waves meet with little resistance) up to 12 miles. If necessary, the message was relayed by drummers across hundreds of miles. This explains why it often happens that all along the route taken by the white man he found that his coming was known well in advance of his arrival.

African drummers are men of status in the community. The technique of playing the drums in such a way as to construct a message is known only to them and is passed on within the family. Several theories have been advanced to explain the mystery of African drum language. It is now generally accepted that the signals are not pre-arranged, but are words in a secret language. So accurate is the drummer's ear and so good his technique that he can make the drum imitate the human voice.

In Europe at that time the drum was used only as a means of communication within an army regiment. Toinot Arbeau, a 16th century French writer, described the use of regimental drums as a "signal and warning to the soldiers to break camp, to advance, to retreat and to give them heart, daring and courage to attack the enemy and to defend themselves with manful vigour."

The horn has also had a limited use throughout man's history as a means of sending simple messages. It kept followers of the hunt informed of the progress of the chase, and it was used in battle. The old French epic poem, the *Chanson de Roland,* tells of the death of Roland at the Battle of Roncesvalles in A.D. 778. In charge of the rearguard of Charlemagne's army, Roland blew on his horn for help when attacked by

Opposite: A French Guards drummer of 1635. *Below:* Horns were also used by newssheet and pamphlet sellers to advertise their wares.

the Saracens. Charlemagne, 30 leagues away, is reported to have heard the blast, but returned too late to save Roland and the rearguard from destruction. The historical facts are different from those of the legend—no warrior called Roland took part in the battle—but the *Chanson* does indicate the importance of the horn for sending messages in battle and the value to an army of a mighty horn blower.

It was not until man learnt more about the use of metal, and could make musical instruments capable of a considerable range of notes, that a refinement of the horn—the bugle—became an essential part of military communications. Around A.D. 1750 the Hanoverian jäger battalions included trained buglers in every regiment, and later in the 18th century an official list of military bugle calls was published in which regimental, routine and field calls were recorded. Today in the army such bugle calls as the Reveille and Last Post are still in use, virtually unchanged in form since the Napoleonic Wars.

One disadvantage of using trumpet and drum calls in warfare was well-known. Recognized and acted upon off the battlefield, they could in the noise and excitement of the battle go unnoticed, especially if the men were inexperienced. Before the charge of the Scots Greys at Waterloo in 1815, the regiment had

The charge of the Scots Greys at Waterloo. They did not hear the sounding of the recall and were cut to pieces.

not seen active service for many years; so only the most senior among officers and men had combat experience. Ordered to charge a French infantry force of 18,000 men, the Scots Greys shattered the enemy and carried on into the French lines. The rally was sounded, but no-one paid any attention. Both horses and men were battle-mad. Nothing could stop them. The regiment charged on through the French position to where 80 enemy guns awaited them. Then, when men and horses were almost exhausted, they were cut off and overwhelmed by heavy French counter-attacks.

When man discovered fire he had another method of communication. For fire could be seen a great distance away if it was lit on an exposed hilltop or on a great plain. And from fire came man's use of smoke, that rose high in the air and therefore could be seen from far away, even across hilly country if the conditions were right. This method was used by the American Indians who became skilled in building smoking fires with damp wood, using a blanket to control the smoke.

There are many examples of fire being used for sending messages. Possibly the best-known in British history—because Lord Macaulay made it the subject of a narrative poem—is the chain of beacons set up in England in 1588 to warn of the approach of the Spanish Armada.

The beacons are lit in July 1588 to warn people of the coming of the Spanish Armada.

Left: The Pharos of Alexandria, built by Ptolemy Soter: the most famous of all lighthouses and one of the wonders of the world. *Right:* The remains of the Roman lighthouse at Dover.

Cossack sentries guarding the border of the old Russian empire used fire beacons built on high wooden platforms to raise the alarm when their outposts were attacked by Mongols or Turks. On seeing the chain of burning fires, the Cossacks armed themselves and rode to an assembly point for a counter-attack on the invaders.

In 1783 during the War of American Independence, when peace was being discussed between the Americans and the British, beacons were built along the banks of the river Hudson. The fires were lit when peace was declared, to let the soldiers know that a cease-fire was to be observed.

Fire beacons were used before the birth of Christ to

mark the entrance to harbours and thus act as a guide to shipping. The centre of trade in the ancient Hellenic world was the eastern Mediterranean. Here the most famous of all harbour beacons was the one on the island of Pharos in the Bay of Alexandria. On top of a 400 feet high square tower a huge wood fire burned day and night, shooting flames into the sky that could be seen 30 miles away in clear weather. Its beacon fire was so well known that in time "pharos" became the word for a beacon or lighthouse.

From the great Pharos of Alexandria, one of the seven wonders of the world, stemmed the lighthouse system now in use all over the world. The first lighthouses were ordinary dwelling houses at the mouth of a harbour. The light came from a coal fire which the lighthouse keeper kept bright with a pair of bellows. The Romans built square towers for lighthouses along the coasts of their Empire. The first in Britain was at Dover, built A.D. 43, now a ruin. Another, built by the Romans at Corunna in northern Spain, is still in use.

As trade increased lighthouses served not only to mark harbours but also to warn shipping of rocks and shoals. In fog the light was rather dim, so sound signals (fog horns) were added which, given the force of steam or electric power, can carry 20 miles. And radio beacons have been installed in some lighthouses to aid ships that have radio-direction finders. Today electric power is the source of light when possible, otherwise incandescent mineral-oil burners or acetylene gas are used. A huge glass lens magnifies the light, using white or red colours that flash off and on.

Once man discovered that certain surfaces reflect sunlight he used the knowledge as a system of communication. The Greeks, Persians and Egyptians all used polished metal as mirrors when necessary. At the battle on the plains of Marathon, the Persians sent news of the progress of the struggle to their ships in Marathon Bay by flashing the sunlight on their shields according to a pre-arranged code.

The eighteenth century Eddystone lighthouse. It was burned down in 1755.

Centuries later, in June 1876, Indian tribes led by Sitting Bull used the same method, this time not with shields but with small mirrors they had obtained from white traders in exchange for furs. From the tops of the Black Mountains overlooking the plain of the Little Big Horn River the Indian tribes exchanged information about their whereabouts and strength, as they closed in on the U.S. cavalry division below. Then they attacked. It was Custer's Last Stand.

In the Second World War the basic principle was still in use. Escape for airmen included polished steel mirrors with a sighting device, so that in an emergency they could aim the signals in any chosen direction.

In the dense forests of the Amazon where sound is deadened by the foliage, explorers found that tribes used vibrations sent through the ground as a means of sending messages.

A pit about 12 inches deep was dug and the bottom was covered with a layer of hard sand, well stamped down. On this rested part of a hollow tree trunk filled with layers of tanned hide and chips of wood, bone and rubber. The trunk was wedged against the side of the pit with springy rubber and wood chips. The tree trunk was then struck by a huge hammer made of wood, hide and rubber, producing sound waves that travelled through the earth. Some distance away at a hearing post an Indian pressed his ear against the top of the tree trunk section, similarly buried, to pick up the vibrations in the ground.

Even whistling has been developed as a means of communication. In Britain it is most in evidence at sheepdog trials where the whistled instructions of the handler are acted upon by the dog in a way that shows how well an intelligent animal can be trained to act on pre-arranged signals. The groundwork of this skill was laid centuries ago by shepherds, who found that a whistle carries more clearly than the human voice in all weathers, and does not call for so much physical effort.

2 : Writing From a Distance

If we look closely at systems of communication we shall see that roughly they are of two kinds. Signals can be used for which the meaning has been pre-arranged. These are the beacon fires giving warning of attack; the bells rung for curfew; the smoke signals; the hand torches; the horn, trumpet, bugle and military drum calls.

The second type does not depend on any pre-arranged signal of a general character. The message can be much more detailed. The most obvious of this type is that of sending a written or spoken message by

A sheepdog acts on whistled instructions from its master—a language it can understand.

some form of transport like a messenger, or a "spoken" message by the secret language of the African drums. An alternative method of sending detailed messages is to build up the words by spelling out the words or letters, as happens in flag and heliograph signalling. The message can be passed on, if necessary, along a chain of transmitting posts until it finally reaches the receiving post at the end of the chain.

Spelling out the letters was done either by fire or flags. The Greeks used both in their system in use about 450 B.C. when flags did the work during the day and torches at night. The Greek alphabet was written out in tabular form with an equal number of letters in a line. Each signal gave the line and the place along that line occupied by the letter, and in this way the word was constructed. The Greeks had a word for this system which persists today—"telegraph" (*telē*—far, *graphē*—a writing) meaning "writing from a distance."

In 1790 a young Frenchman, Claude Chappé, applied the same principle in a different form and produced the Chappé optical telegraph. It was a rather clumsy construction. A long pole had movable bars—a transverse arm with shorter arms at each end—attached to the top. By manipulating guide ropes, the bars could be arranged in nearly 80 positions representing the letters of the alphabet, combined consonants such as "ch" and "sh", punctuation marks and numbers. It was not a simple method, for to get the message across land, a number of fairly tall transmitting posts had to be built to enable the signalling bars to be plainly seen at a distance. This was a costly business.

It was not until 1793, after three years' dogged perseverence by Chappé, that the French Republican Government finally tested the invention and gave him the go-ahead. Immediately a large scale building programme was started. Between Paris and Lille 22 telegraph stations were built to span the 130 miles between the two cities.

The first official message announced the capture of Condé by the Republic in its fight against opponents who were trying to reverse the success of the French Revolution. In three-quarters of an hour a very typical official reply came from the city leaders of Lille, congratulating the Republic on its triumphs.

The speed and accuracy with which the message had been sent and answered impressed the Government, and other lines of optical telegraph communication stations were built. A message from Paris to Strasbourg took six minutes to reach the receiving end; to Brest, a distance of 365 miles, seven minutes. Improvements followed. By equipping the staff of the transmitting stations with telescopes for reading the distant signals, the stations could be built much further away from each other.

The system slowly aroused interest in other European countries. Sweden built one in 1793. Denmark, Prussia and Austria followed. Russia waited almost half a century before adopting the invention, but then covered 950 miles from St. Petersburg to Warsaw with 48 stations.

England preferred to go it alone, and from 1795 onwards experimented with a similar optical system invented by Lord George Murray. This had 12 small swinging doors fixed in a scaffold surround. Each letter was represented by a special combination of open and closed doors. Like Chappé's telegraph it performed quite well except during mist or fog, and at night. Britain finally abandoned Murray's invention in 1816, but the Chappé system lasted another 50 years.

Meanwhile man's thirst for knowledge was urging

Nelson's famous signal to the fleet at Trafalgar.

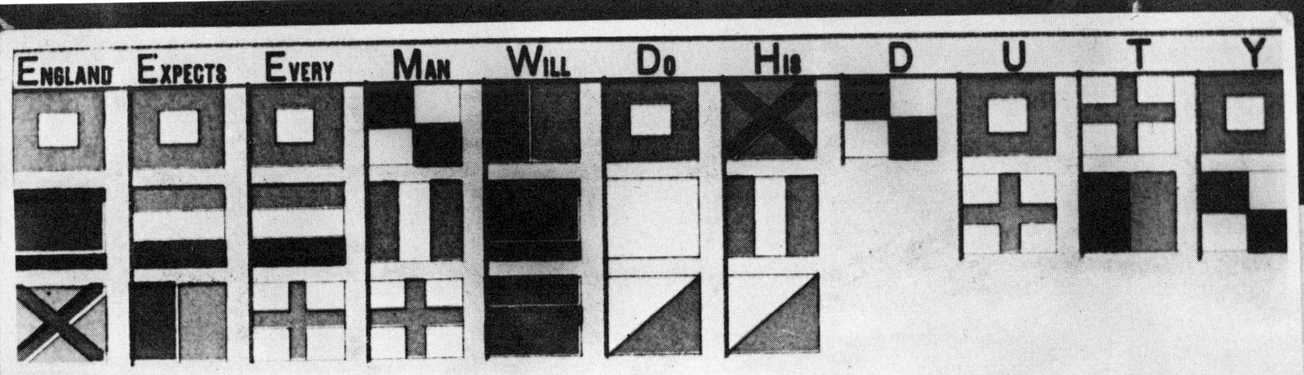

A signaller sends messages to German ships arriving at Ösel, Russia, in November 1917.

inventors to find a way of spelling out the letters of the alphabet in a less clumsy way which could operate in the night and through mist and fog. Electricity, the new source of energy, provided the answer.

The respect shown to flags in such traditional ceremonies as the Trooping of the Colour indicates the part they have played in military history. They served as a means of identification for tribes, regiments and armies, and in battle became a rallying point.

Identification was also the purpose of flags flown by ships. Around 1570 an ensign of standard design came into use by English vessels. It had the Cross of St. George in the cauton (a rectangular section of the flag in the upper corner near the staff) and the remainder consisted of horizontal stripes that, according to their number, indicated the home port of the vessel. This later fell into disuse and Red, White and Blue Ensigns were flown to designate ships of the three colour squadrons. Since 1874 the Red Ensign has been flown by ships of the Merchant Navy, the Blue Ensign by ships of the Naval Reserve and the White Ensign by ships of the Royal Navy and the Royal Yacht Squadron.

Signalling by flags was common between ships of the same nationality, but no international code of signals was drawn up until 1817 when some 9,000 signals, to be made by various combinations of flags, were established. Today the International Code, by means of a set of pre-agreed signals, appears in eight languages—English, French, Italian, German, Japanese, Norwegian, Russian and Greek. Ships can communicate with each other, using the code, without a knowledge of the language of the other participating countries. Some 650 two-flag and 15,600 three-flag messages are available.

But the International Code is only one of many methods of communication between ships at sea, developed in response to varying conditions and the distance between vessels. The choice of which to use depends on circumstances. Sailors can signal by Morse

Code or semaphore, using flags; they can signal by Morse using a flashing light, buzzer (radiotelegraphy), foghorn, whistle or siren; or they can use their own voices through a loud hailer or by radio telephone.

Man has put to good use a characteristic he observed many thousands of years ago in the homing pigeon. Because this bird is monogamous—it mates for life—it has an instinctive drive to return to its nest and partner. If taken from the nest it will fly back there when freed by means of its homing instinct and an inborn ability to find its bearings by the sun. Although the distance from which it can fly home is not very great in a wild bird, with training it is possible to have a domestic pigeon that can find its way home from 1,200 miles away. The Egyptians had an extensive pigeon messenger-service in 3000 B.C., pigeon lofts being built at 5-mile intervals along important routes. So too did the Babylonians, Greeks and Romans.

A pigeon-messenger was used by Nathan Rothschild, the banker, to bring him the news of the outcome of the battle of Waterloo in 1815. This was just one message of many, for throughout the Napoleonic Wars his agents with the opposing armies had kept him informed by pigeon-messenger of the turn of events—information which enabled him to become the richest banker in the world.

In modern times, and in spite of the existence of such sophisticated methods as telegraphy and radio communication, the pigeon has proved invaluable. If, in time of war, telegraph wires have been destroyed, or radio silence has to be observed, then a homing pigeon can take the message. In the Korean War in 1950, pigeons were part of the equipment of American parachute troops landing behind enemy lines. For a period of four months all messages sent by pigeon from seven such groups were safely received.

When Paris was besieged by the Germans in 1870 after the defeat of Napoleon III at Sedan, an airmail service for letters was devised, using balloons. To get

Balloons leaving besieged Paris in the winter of 1871. Balloons and pigeon post were the only way of keeping in touch with the rest of France.

letters back into Paris was a problem, for there was no guarantee that incoming balloons would escape German riflemen or could land accurately inside the besieged city. Then someone thought of homing pigeons. They had been used by the Dutch at the sieges of Haarlem in 1573 and Leyden in the following year in the war against the Spanish. These useful birds were now sent out of Paris in the balloons that took the letters. Wherever the balloons landed in unoccupied France the birds were taken to a central despatch base at Tours. Here messages for Paris were written out and attached to the birds. The homing instinct guided them back to their lofts in Paris. As a precaution the pigeons were released in groups of five, each bird carrying copies of the same despatches.

An even more efficient system was then invented by photographers, who photographed the messages, and reduced them to microfilm. More than 2,500 messages on each of two dozen films could be carried by one pigeon. Under stress of siege, man had improvised and improved communication to a surprising degree. The pigeon post to Paris was reported as a triumph in newspapers all over the western world. The pigeon messenger, with a message written on light-weight paper and clipped to its leg, is a direct link between us and the remote past, so efficient as to be in use in 3000 B.C. and today.

This serves to remind us that the history of communications is not an orderly procession of one method following on another. At all times, several methods were in use, depending on the circumstances, the distance to be covered, the length of the message and the obstacles existing between sender and recipient.

3: The Early Messengers

If one had to say which was the most important development in the whole history of man, it would probably be the invention of a written language. It has enabled people to put their thoughts into words and so preserve them for reference in books where they can be read by other people, enabling knowledge to be passed on from generation to generation and from one nation to another. About 3,000 years ago the Phoenicians perfected a system of writing using 22 pictures, each representing a sound, so that any word could be made up. The Romans adapted the Phoenician system, and our English alphabet is based on the Roman.

It is possible to put written communications into two categories. There are those intended for future reference, chiefly books, but also journals and magazines whose contents are of a high quality. The second category takes in all the millions of messages necessary in everyday life. Some of these take the form of messages, either business or personal; some take the form of newspaper and magazine reports and articles; some are no more than announcements that a jumble sale will be held in the school hall next Saturday morning.

Even these day-to-day communications can turn out to be important enough to be collected together and published. We get letters of famous men and women, reprinted in book form, that are referred to time and time again. The letters of Florence Nightin-

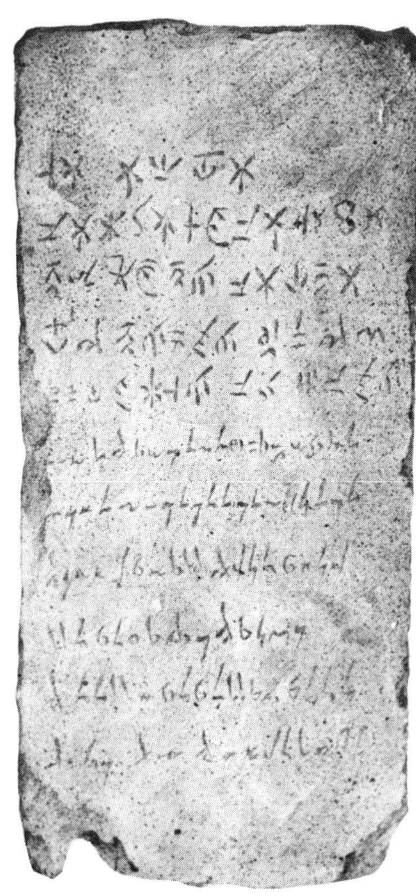

The top six lines of this inscription are in Phoenician, from which all western alphabets come. The rest is in ancient Cypriot.

The Greek messenger
Pheidippides arrives in Sparta.

gale from the Crimea are an example. They give an insight into the workings of the military mind, the army organization, the place of women in society and other topics which are of great interest to social and military historians of later generations.

Until about the eleventh century, when the large monastic establishments and universities began to revive European culture, the great majority of written communications were concerned with affairs of immediate importance, the details of everyday life. In particular they dealt with military and civil matters arising out of conquest and the maintenance of order in conquered regions.

Detailed messages had, of course, to be written, but a short message was committed to memory by the messenger and passed on by word of mouth. For some reason the spoken message makes a greater impact than a written one. Poets and writers sense this appeal, hence many of the incidents that have become part of the folk-lore of history have been made so by subsequent dramatic tellings of the story and its appearance in printed form.

So there is an element of chance in which stories we inherit from the past and which we do not. Thanks to

Paul Revere's midnight ride.

Herodotus, the Greek historian, we have a great deal of information about the systems of communication in the Mediterranean region from the 7th to the 4th centuries B.C. He tells the story of Pheidippides the Greek messenger, who in 490 B.C. ran 140 miles from Athens to Sparta to ask for help in repelling the Persian invaders whose fleet had anchored in the Bay of Marathon. Pheidippides reached Sparta after running for a day and a night.

Another legendary story of that time tells of the Greek victory over the Persians at Marathon. The same messenger Pheidippedes ran non-stop from the battlefield to Athens, shouted "Victory!" (*Nike!*) and fell dead from exhaustion. This incident is the inspiration of the Marathon in the modern Olympic games.

Many messengers have carried vital information, but they are forgotten. It takes some kind of record, an historian's note, an epic poem, or a ballad passed down from singer to singer, to get a deed remembered. But for Macaulay's poem on the Armada not many people would know where the warning beacons were sited.

Were it not for Longfellow's poem *The Midnight*

Ride of Paul Revere, it is doubtful if Revere's fame would have spread beyond America, for in all he covered no more than 16 miles—but the message he carried helped to change the history of the world.

It happened in America in 1775, when British troops moved to capture arms horded by the discontented American colonists. The arms were stored in the little towns of Concord and Lexington, less than 20 miles from Boston. On 18th April the British closed all roads from Boston to the two towns. A British battleship sailed up the mouth of the River Charles from Boston Bay to prevent anyone crossing the river by the ferry from Boston to Charlestown on the other bank.

Paul Revere, a silversmith by trade, a leader of the colonists and a fine horseman, saw the preparations being made, guessed their purpose and set out to warn the inhabitants of Concord and Lexington of the danger. At night he crossed the river in a rowing boat, going a long way seaward of the battleship to escape detection. In Charlestown he was given a good horse and rode out into the country. Almost immediately a British officer saw him and gave chase, but Revere soon threw him off. Through Medford, Menotomy and on to Lexington he rode, hammering on the door of every homestead along the route to shout his warning, "The Redcoats are out!" At Lexington two other horsemen joined him for the final ride to Concord. They split up to make more certain that one would get through the British troops posted outside the town. This proved a wise move. Three miles from Lexington Paul Revere was captured, and then one of his companions. The third man got through to Concord in time to prevent the bulk of the arms being taken by the British.

The colonists whom Revere had alerted gathered at Lexington, armed themselves and prepared to resist the British soldiers. In the early morning light of 19th April shots were exchanged between the colonists and the British. The War of American Independence had begun. The name of Revere's two companions—one

Hammurabi, king of Babylon. The writing asks a goddess to look after the king's life.

of whom roused the colonists of Concord—are forgotten. Revere and his message are remembered because Longfellow made Revere the central character of a narrative poem.

The messenger service first existed around the shores of the Mediterranean—Egypt, Palestine, Asia Minor and south-west Asia—where successive empires had gradually developed quite a high degree of civilization. Writing and reading were practised by the well-to-do, a coinage was established and calculating methods were invented. But the lifeblood of the empires was conquest; in turn the Babylonians, the Assyrians, Persians, Greeks and Romans dominated the known world by force. This is why much of the story of communications in the ancient world concerns military affairs.

The life of the solitary messenger was not a happy one, although it had some prestige. A piece of Egyptian clay from about 2300 B.C. tells of the perils of the job: "Before departing he maketh over his fortune to his children for fear of the Asiatics and the wild animals. Scarce hath he returned home but he must set forth again." Sometimes the runner carried homing pigeons which he released if he was in danger of an attack by robbers. When the pigeons returned home, other messengers were sent out with the same message.

The Greeks selected their messengers for short or long runs. Service as a long distance runner was the more precarious of the two. There was the physical strain, and there was always the chance of being killed or injured. The runners were given some protection; their rulers let it be known that anyone harming or hindering a messenger would be severely punished. They were given means of identification so that there could be no excuse about not knowing who the messenger was.

When they carried a written message, the Greek runners had the message itself, written on papyrus tape and wound round a stick, as proof of identity. The Roman messengers carried a piece of insignia—

A Greek runner.

Mercury, the messenger
of the Roman gods.

just as a Rolls Royce has a flying lady on its bonnet—in the form of a short staff adorned with goose wings. This can be seen in drawings and statues of Mercury, the messenger of the gods in Roman mythology.

It is not easy to compare the efficiency of the messenger services of the ancient empires; a great deal depended on the degree of law and order the conquerors had been able to establish in the lands they overran, and on the length of time they had occupied those territories. We do know that as far back as the 19th century B.C. the Assyrians had a very efficient messenger service working for them. Clay tablets found at Kanesh, south of the Black Sea, indicate how much Assyrian merchants relied on it. Asking for an answer "by return of post," a phrase that occurs on several of these tablets, might well have been taken from a business letter written today, and suggests that there was a regular schedule of deliveries.

In the 6th century B.C., when the Assyrian Empire was at its most powerful, the king at Nineveh maintained contact, by means of the postal service, with governors of conquered territories such as Tarsus, Sidon, Memphis and Susa in what are now Turkey, Lebanon, Egypt and West Iran.

Herodotus, the Greek historian mentioned earlier, writes about the Persian Empire in the 5th century B.C. which was bigger than that of Assyria. The Persians concentrated on building and maintaining a network of roads to allow troops and messengers to travel rapidly along the main trade routes. What Herodotus calls royal stations, to accommodate messengers and horses, had been built on these roads. Between the capital Susa (West Iran) and Sardis (Turkey), a distance of 328 parasangs, there were 81 stations at approximately 16-mile intervals.

Cyrus the Great, who died in 529 B.C., laid the foundation of this service; under him only excellent riders who possessed stamina and perseverence were made couriers. "Neither snow nor rain nor sun nor heat nor gloom of night stays these couriers from the swift completion of their appointed rounds,'' wrote Herodotus admiringly.

This system became part of army procedure in time of war. Xerxes, the Persian emperor who ruled in the fifth century B.C., established courier posts along the route of his armies, horses and men being stationed about one day's journey from each other. He used this system to send back word of his defeat by the Greeks at Salamis in 480 B.C., while the Greeks on the other side were still using the long and short distance runner service.

Verse 10, chapter 8 of the book of Esther in the Bible mentions this Persian communication system; Xerxes is called by the Hebrew name of Ahasuerus, and the capital Susa is called Shushan. We are told that the couriers rode on mules, camels and young dromedaries as well as horses. There is another reference to the royal postal system in the Second Book of Chronicles, chapter 30 verse 6.

The first written messages took the form of a series of pictures—a *pictograph*—on soft clay tablets, drawn with a wedge-shaped stylus. The Sumerians developed this cuneiform writing 5,000 years ago; between 2500 and 2000 B.C. the Phoenicians and Assyrians modified it and produced a phonetic alphabet. From cuneiform tablets discovered by archaeologists it is clear that quite complex messages were sent by this means, and that the tablets were subsequently kept for reference just as we file important letters and documents today.

Below: An example of cuneiform text.

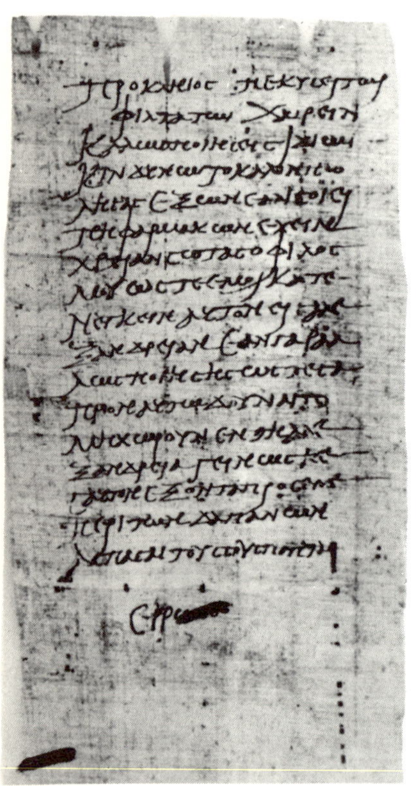

A Greek papyrus letter.

The Egyptians had a messenger system for official communications from about 2000 B.C., although there were private messenger services and many merchants used their slaves. A better writing material than clay tablets had been discovered by the Egyptians around 2400 B.C. This was papyrus, a sheet made from reed fibres. It was not easy to write hieroglyphics on it, so a new more flowing style of writing was invented suitable for papyrus and a reed pen. The use of hieroglyphics gradually died out, until it was kept only for religious writings and architectural inscriptions.

The manufacture of papyrus gradually became a major Egyptian industry and for some 3,000 years after its invention it remained the standard writing material of the Mediterranean region. The Romans used it for writing letters, preferring it to the old method of writing with metal or ivory styluses on wax-coated tablets, but they still used the tablets when papyrus could not be obtained.

The Roman Empire was larger than Persia's; it included all of Europe, the Near East and North Africa, and in its heyday more than 9,000 miles of road had been constructed. The Romans followed the Persian system of building messenger posts along important routes; but they developed a far more complicated postal system than the Persians ever had, and in the first century B.C., when the Romans conquered Britain, that system was in operation in the rest of the Empire. Post houses were built a day's horse ride from each other; between these were intermediate resting places where the animals could be changed and fed, and repairs carried out to carts and harness. In addition to the swift letter post manned by horsemen, the Romans introduced a parcel post service using carts pulled by horses, mules or oxen.

A department under the direction of the Postmaster General ran the messenger service. The postmasters lived in the large and comfortable post houses, and the lesser officials at the smaller intermediate resting places.

Grooms, wheelmakers, carpenters and harness makers, together with foot soldiers, made up the complement of personnel at these stations along the route.

The horse messengers did not take a single letter as some of the ancient Greek runners did. This would happen rarely, only when urgent news had to get through in the fastest possible time—100 miles in a day is the fastest recorded. Most letters were collected and sorted and sent in bags to particular destinations— the Uttoxeter bag, the York bag, and so on. The messenger might have two horses, one for riding, the other carrying the letter bags. Here the pace was more leisurely—about 5 miles an hour and between 30 and 50 miles a day.

The Romans were strict about who used the imperial postal system; the messenger services dealt only with official letters, and the post-chaises and carts were intended only for officials and high ranking soldiers and their baggage. Private letters had to be sent by other means. So all over the Empire private companies sprang up providing carriages and animals for hire, and many men worked as messengers or for messenger companies.

After the Romans had left Britain in the fifth century A.D. the communication system fell into disuse. Many of the roads became overgrown and disappeared from view, to be laid bare again many centuries later. Some were destroyed and the stones used for building houses or walls. Some became no more than landmarks to indicate a boundary, as Watling Street became the border between Alfred the Great's kingdom and that of Guthrum the Dane. All over Europe travel was restricted and trade declined.

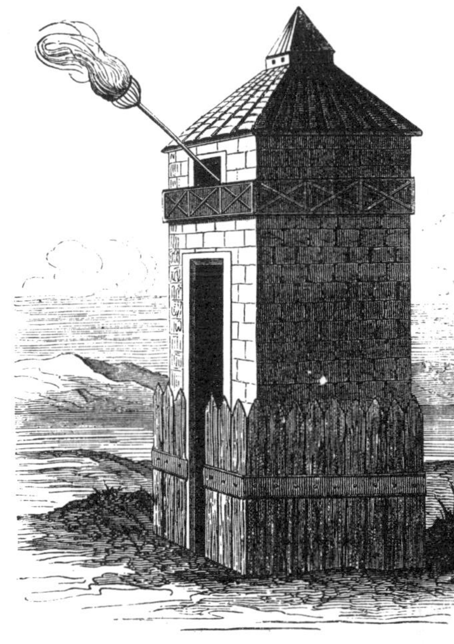

Signalling with a flaming torch from post to post on a Roman road.

B

Above: A messenger brings a letter to the French king's army. *Below:* A state carriage, illustrated on a manuscript.

4: The English Revival

It was around the courts of the kings of England that the postal system slowly grew again. Henry I (1100–1135) established a service of King's Messengers; they had the best horses possible. King John (1199–1216) fitted them out in the royal livery. Edward I (1272–1307) copied parts of the Roman postal system and established post houses along a few major routes, where horses were stabled for the messengers. Henry IV (1399–1413) did more. He used lodging houses and inns to stable the horses for the postboys, and also gave the messengers the right to travel through private property if it was quicker.

During a war with Scotland in 1481 Edward IV extended the post house system—with about 20 miles between posts—along the main route to the north of England. This service stayed, for people travelling north on state business, long after the war ended.

But the postal service in England remained extremely limited. It was much worse, for example, than the excellent service built up in China under Kubla Khan, about which Marco Polo wrote so enthusiastically in the 13th century. Here 300,000 horses were in service throughout the 10,000 post stations of the empire. In the 15th century the Ming emperor Yung Lo opened the imperial postal service to civilians as well.

This was unheard of in England. Members of monasteries and universities, lawyers and merchants who

A contemporary illustration of a Stuart foot postman.

wished to send correspondence in or out of England had to find ways of their own, for the royal messenger service was strictly for court correspondence. European traders in Britain agreed to take letters abroad in their ships, a service which became known as the Strangers' Post. People used any travellers who happened to be passing. There is a record of £10 paid to two friars in 1430 who brought letters from Paris to London. Ordinary folk chanced their luck of letters being delivered by giving them to servants and strangers. From this custom the private carrying of letters became a means of livelihood.

The importance of the royal messenger service grew as government became more complex, and Henry VIII's quarrel with the Pope considerably swelled the number of letters sent during the first half of the 16th century. Henry created the position of Master of the Posts and appointed Sir Brian Tuke to be the first holder of the office. As well as maintaining the relay system of post houses along such important routes as London to Dover and London to Scotland, Tuke organized temporary routes so that "wherever the King is, posts are laid from London to his Grace." The men who carried the mail in saddle-bags were called postboys. They announced their coming by blowing on a post horn, and managed an average speed of about five miles an hour in winter, and seven in summer.

The court intrigues which marked the reign of Queen Elizabeth I were dependent on letters passing between conspirators. Although Mary Queen of Scots had been imprisoned by Elizabeth, she went on writing to the Spanish ambassador and friends abroad. She used many tricks to hide the letters from her jailers; they were concealed in books, in shoes, even in waterproof coverings inside kegs of beer. In 1591, to stop the flow of treasonable correspondence, Elizabeth made it an offence for anyone to carry letters other than the official postmen. So private letters went by the state postal service for the first time. But the new law could not be enforced, for many merchants had their own ships and used them to operate a letter service.

Elizabeth appointed Thomas Randolph to be her Master of Posts. He made the towns on post routes responsible for supplying relief horses. This was much resented as often all the horses in the district had other work to do, and on occasion even the ploughing had to stop while the plough horses were taken to carry the royal mail to the next post house.

It is doubtful if the day-to-day posts arrived any faster than they had 500 years before. But the relay system meant that urgent messages could be taken 100 miles in a day. When Elizabeth died, Sir Robert Carey rode from London to take the news to James VI of Scotland. He left London at 9 a.m. on the 25th March 1603 and arrived in Edinburgh in the late evening of the 27th, covering a distance of 400 miles at an average of about 7 m.p.h.

Later, the state postal service tried to attract private letters. James I re-affirmed in 1609 the proclamation made by Elizabeth in 1591 about mail sent abroad. The Master of Posts imposed a fixed charge for inland domestic letters and organised a cross-channel postal service. The merchants continued to flout the law by sending mail on their own ships, and this quarrel went on for almost half a century until the State finally won.

The postal service got better after reorganization in 1635. A scale of charges was introduced for domestic mail, and people posted and collected letters at the nearest post house. It was another 45 years before mail was delivered to the front door.

The inland postal charges in 1635 were:

Bookbinding: illustrations from a 1659 book.

Distance	Pence per single sheet letter	Pence per double sheet letter	Pence per ounce
Up to 80 miles	2	4	6
From 80 to 140 miles	4	8	9
More than 140 miles	6	12	12

In 1657 Cromwell, the Lord Protector, upgraded the position of Master of the Posts to that of Postmaster General; and a few years later, to make the service more efficient, a date stamp for letters was introduced: "A stamp is invented that is putt upon every letter shewing the day of the month that every letter comes to the office, so that no letter carryer may dare to detayne a letter from post to post, which before was usual."

At that time about 50 people were employed in the London post offices. During the Great Plague they aired letters over vinegar, mistakenly believing this would kill any infection carried by them. 30 postmen died in the Plague.

In 1680 William Dockwra tried to break the state monopoly by establishing the London Penny Post. He recruited nearly 500 people all over London to act as local postmasters. Each district had its own sorting office, and business areas had no less than 12 deliveries a day! Dockwra made a good profit out of the idea.

Later the government took over his system and the

Part of a writing master's copy sheet, of about 1600. The elaborate initial at the front is a C.

The first London to Bath and Bristol mail coach of 1785.

man himself, because of his obvious talent, was made Comptroller of the Penny Post.

So successful was the now legal London Penny Post that, following pressure from other towns, an Act was finally passed in 1765 to allow any town to set up its own penny post. By 1840 more than 350 towns in England and Wales had done so. But it still cost a lot more to send a letter outside the town.

Travel by coach began in the reign of Elizabeth I, but the bad state of the roads right up to the end of the 18th century made this type of transport difficult, and pedestrians, cattle and horsemen were the principal road users. Coaches were little more than waggons with seats for passengers, and there were no springs until 1754. Travelling on any road was uncomfortable. The Romans built good roads from military necessity, and it was the Jacobite Rebellion in 1745 that caused an improvement in the main roads from London to the north. Later, trade led to the improvement of other main roads. The turnpike system (whereby travellers helped to pay for road repairs) brought about a general raising of road standards from 1773 onwards.

One result of road improvements was that along some routes the stage coaches were going faster than the post-boys. In 1753 a 160-mile coach journey from Shrewsbury to London took 4 days in winter (fare 18 shillings) and $3\frac{1}{2}$ days in summer (fare 21 shillings—you paid more for a quicker journey!). This worked out at about 4 miles an hour in winter. The first mail coach—with the royal coat of arms on the door panels—ran from London to Bristol in 1785 and covered the 119 miles at a speed of seven miles per hour. At this speed some people thought there was a risk to health and pessimists talked about people dying from infection of the brain brought about by fast travel.

Here are comparative times for the London to Edinburgh journey:

1550	Post horse service	12 days summer
		20 days winter
1650	Stage coach	13 days summer
1750	Stage coach	10 days summer
		12 days winter
1776	"Flying coach"	4 days
1800	Mail coach	3 days 2 nights
1832	Mail coach	42 hours 33 minutes

Within a few years of the introduction of mail coaches in 1785 all post was carried by coach to the principal towns.

Employees were made aware of the importance of their work. It became a point of honour to "get the post through!" So strong was this that it brought tragedy to the driver and guard on the Dumfries–Edinburgh run in February 1831. The coach became stuck in a snow drift. The two men took the mailbags

and rode forward on two of the horses to the next post
house, where they were joined by an ostler. The snow
became deeper and the horses were stuck, so the ostler
returned to the post house with them. Driver and guard
struggled forward on foot towards Edinburgh, carrying
the mailbags. But some days later they were found
frozen to death in a snowdrift.

The big increase in trade from 1800 to 1850 led
industrialists to look for a speedier and more reliable
transport system than that provided by the roads and
canals. So they built railways. And in 1830 the Post
Office, always on the alert to improve its service,
began sending letters and parcels by train. The first
consignment went on the Manchester–Liverpool line,
and averaging 20 miles an hour about halved the time
it would have taken by mail coach. More and more mail
was then transferred from road to rail as the railway
network spread.

The last daily run of a mail coach from London took
place in 1846, when the London–Newmarket–Norwich
service closed down. On cross-country journeys not

The mail coach stuck in a drift
of snow.

served by rail, and in remote areas like Cornwall, Ireland and Scotland, the mail coach went on. But its life had been a short one—a mere 60 years in all—and it ended, ironically, when the nation's roads were getting better and better.

Putting up the price of sending a letter through the mail—as happened often during the Napoleonic wars —was, of course, a great hardship to all except the well-to-do middle and upper classes, and people thought up many ways of avoiding payment. In the first chapter there was a distinction made between signals that had a pre-arranged meaning and communications that gave information in detail. Now letters are very clearly the latter kind, but the high cost of the postal service during the wars with the French forced people to use them as pre-arranged signals whenever they could.

Letters in those days were paid for on delivery. So a man who was going on a journey would arrange to send a letter as soon as he got there, telling his wife he had arrived safely. When the letter was delivered the wife refused to pay the charge—but having recognized the handwriting she knew her husband had sent it. Detailed information could be sent in this way— coloured inks or squiggles or diagrams on the outside of the letter giving the message in code. Illegal carriers of mail so flourished that in time the letters they carried outnumbered those sent through the Post Office. It is said that when the regular Liverpool–New York steamship service opened, only five letters were in the official Post Office bag. Yet the same ship was illegally carrying 10,000 letters!

5: The Modern Post Office

The opposition to the high postal charges was led by Rowland Hill. Hill pointed out that the method of paying for the letter when it was delivered was wasteful because every year people refused many thousands of letters which littered the post offices—and much energy and time had been spent in getting them to their destination. Instead he suggested that the sender should pay a small fee according to letter weight; in this way no letter would be handled unless the Post Office first got its fee.

Hill had seen how the high rates had caused misery to the poor. He wrote: "I early saw the inconvenience of being poor . . . she (my mother) was afraid the post-man might bring a letter while she had no money to pay postage."

Another new idea of Hill's was to have stamped envelopes and adhesive stamps, and he suggested having letter boxes where mail could be "posted" for collection—a system already in use in Paris.

So Hill introduced both stick-on postage stamps and post boxes. His proposals were a great success, and a uniform post—one penny per half ounce—for the whole of the country started on 10th January 1840.

The first gummed stamp to be used was the now-famous Penny Black. It did not bear the name of the country of origin; as no other countries had stamps at that time, it could only be British. This tradition still

The first post box.

Above: The Penny Black, the first adhesive stamp issued in Britain, 1840. *Below:* A London postman with his bell.

continues. Nor was the stamp perforated; the process was not developed until 1854. The man who collected the letters—he carried a locked bag with a slit in it and rang a bell to announce his presence—continued to do the job until about 1852 when pillar-boxes began to be put up all over the country. The success of the penny post led to its introduction in other countries, the earliest being the U.S.A. in 1845 and Canada and France in 1849.

Hill at first was criticized by the rich and important. The Postmaster General, Lord Lichfield, said "Of all the wild and visionary schemes I have ever heard or read of, it is the most extravagant." Yet this "wild" scheme more than doubled the number of letters sent in the year following the introduction of the penny post.

For centuries only the rich and powerful had been able to send and receive mail; when the service was made available to all in the eighteenth century the postal charges had been increased so much that all advantage to the poorer classes was lost, the rates being beyond their means. It was the support given by the common people for postal reform that forced the adoption of Hill's proposals in spite of the opposition of reluctant statesmen. The introduction of the penny post was part of a general movement, which included political representation and education, to extend privileges hitherto enjoyed only by the well-to-do to the poorer people.

To prevent the smuggling of correspondence by ships—because the Post Office service itself was so expensive—an Act of Parliament in 1711 made it illegal to send letters by private ships to places where packets (fast government ships carrying mail) were in service. To make the postal service more attractive four fast packets were built in 1755, each of 200 tons and with a crew of 30, and armed against attacks by the French, to ply from Falmouth to New York. But in spite of these attempts to suppress the illegal carrying

of mail it was not until the penny post was introduced in 1840 that it ceased.

As soon as steamships showed themselves to be fast and reliable the Post Office used them, especially on ocean routes. The Dutch ship *Curaçao* made the first all-steam crossing from Rotterdam to the West Indies in 1827. In 1833 the Atlantic crossing was made in 25 days, and then improvements in design and engine power made crossings faster and faster. The *Sirius* arrived at New York after a record 18 days in 1838; but this triumph was short-lived. The *Great Western* arrived a few hours later, having crossed in 15 days. This paddle-driven ship was built of wood. A change from wood to iron and from paddle to screw then took place in shipbuilding; in 1843 the *Great Britain*, made of iron and screw-driven, cut the time of the Atlantic crossing to 14 days. Another half-century and the

HM Packet *Granville* is attacked by three American privateers off Barbados, 1777. There was still considerable danger in travelling by sea.

Cunard liner *Lucania* was doing it in 6½ days. Today liners on the Atlantic crossing, carrying surface mail, can do the journey in 4 days. The Cunarder *Queen Mary* holds the British record of 3 days 15 hours, set in 1946; the American and world record is held by the *United States*, which took 3 days and 10 hours in 1952.

On routes to the Far East and Australia steamships were slower to take over from sail. Coaling stations were far apart and the two or three days the steamships had to spend on coaling on the way gave the sailing ships an advantage. Clippers engaged in the China tea trade and in competition with each other had speeded the mails to and from China. The *Oriental*, an American clipper, sailed from Hong Kong to London in 97 days in 1850; this was an astonishing time and nothing near it was recorded until sixteen years later when three clippers engaged in the tea trade, but also carrying mail from the Far East, sailed from Foochow in China to London in 99 days.

But, as more coaling stations were established along the routes, the steamships proved faster; so the mail was sent by them. The opening of the Suez Canal in

1869 was the final blow to sail. The large sailing ships found it impossible to navigate the Canal.

The reform of the postal service coincided with a dramatic growth in the construction of railways. Steam power on rails seemed to excite the population much more than air power did when it arrived a century later. Much of the public esteem that the Post Office gathered in the second half of the nineteenth century was due to the service provided by the railways in the swift transport of mail.

Opposition to the railways was quite strong at first from canal and coach companies, and farmers. But people with influence in Parliament were given "expenses" to get railway bills through in the 1830's and 1840's, and so Parliamentary corruption hastened the improvement of the Post Office service. Queen Victoria finally set the seal on the popularity of the railways when she travelled from Paddington to Windsor. Originally she had decided to make this a one-way trip, but the speed, safety and comfort of the journey so impressed her that she made the return journey the same way.

First and second class carriages on the Liverpool and Manchester railway.

The Post Office had already assessed the value of the railways for mail-carrying before Rowland Hill's reforms. By an arrangement with the Grand Junction Railway Company a special Travelling Post Office Van had been built from a horse box, and it came into service on the Birmingham to Liverpool line in 1838. Fast trains took $4\frac{1}{2}$ hours for the 98-mile journey, slower ones from 5 to $5\frac{1}{2}$. Compare these with the mail coach times of 12 to 13 hours; the difference made the union of Post Office and rail transport inevitable.

In its modest way this travelling sorting office was the forerunner of the Travelling Post Office "Specials" —trains that operate every night carrying nothing but mail which is collected, sorted and deposited en route. The T.P.O. linking London with Aberdeen leaves Euston at 20.20 hours, arriving at its destination at 09.11 hours; that linking London with Penzance leaves Paddington at 22.30 hours, arriving at its destination at 06.30 hours. No other form of mail

The inland letter office of the General Post Office, 1844.

delivery can compare with this for all-round service, bearing in mind that mail is taken aboard and dropped off at all major towns and cities on the way.

The speed of the postal service is tied to rail speeds, for today the railways are the backbone of the service in Britain, just as shipping routes and airlines are its links with the rest of the world.

Although the trains replaced mail coaches on the main routes they could not take over on cross-country journeys and in remote rural areas. Here the horse-drawn vehicles continued to operate. The introduction of the parcel post in 1883 underlined the usefulness of the horse for pulling loaded vans over rough country roads, but as the century drew to its close the motor van began to make its appearance. Now the Post Office has about 60,000 motor vehicles ranging from articulated lorries to mini-vans. The majority are the small vans used for collecting the post from letter boxes and for delivering the parcel post.

The first scheduled London to Paris flight carried the first air mail letters from Britain in 1919.

In America, horse-drawn mail played a much greater part in that vast country's communication system than in Britain. The Pony Express and Wells Fargo stage coaches united the east and west sides of the U.S.A., and were still in operation over some major routes long after the railways had taken over the major routes in Britain. For those areas within the British Isles that are separated from the mainland by water, mail was once taken by boat. Today the airplane can do the work quicker. In 1934 a mail air service was started between Inverness and the Orkneys. Later the post to the Channel Isles and Eire was speeded by this means, and since 1961 Edinburgh and Belfast have been linked by air.

The first British postal service by air was on the London to Paris flight in 1919. Letters cost two shillings and sixpence ($12\frac{1}{2}$p.) an ounce. However, the very first scheduled air-mail route was in the U.S.A. This was in 1918, from Washington to New York. Regular air mail services all over the world were developed from about 1925 onwards. The London to India route was opened in 1929, and five years later air mail from London to Australia started. A letter by air from London to Bombay today takes $2\frac{1}{2}$ days, by surface mail (sea) 14 days; air mail London to Sydney takes 7 days, by sea 32 days.

Another invention—the lighter-than-air airship—was at first favourably regarded as a possible way of improving the overseas mail service. But it turned out not to be reliable enough.

These airships, or *dirigibles* as they are sometimes called, were used for occasional mail-carrying duties between the two World Wars. In July 1919 the British *R 34* made the first successful round trip from East Fortune in Scotland to Roosevelt Field, New York, but no regular service was developed. It was left to Germany to establish a regular service. Her airships made 172 Atlantic crossings between 1928 and 1936, the *Graf Zeppelin* and the *Hindenburg* carrying mail to

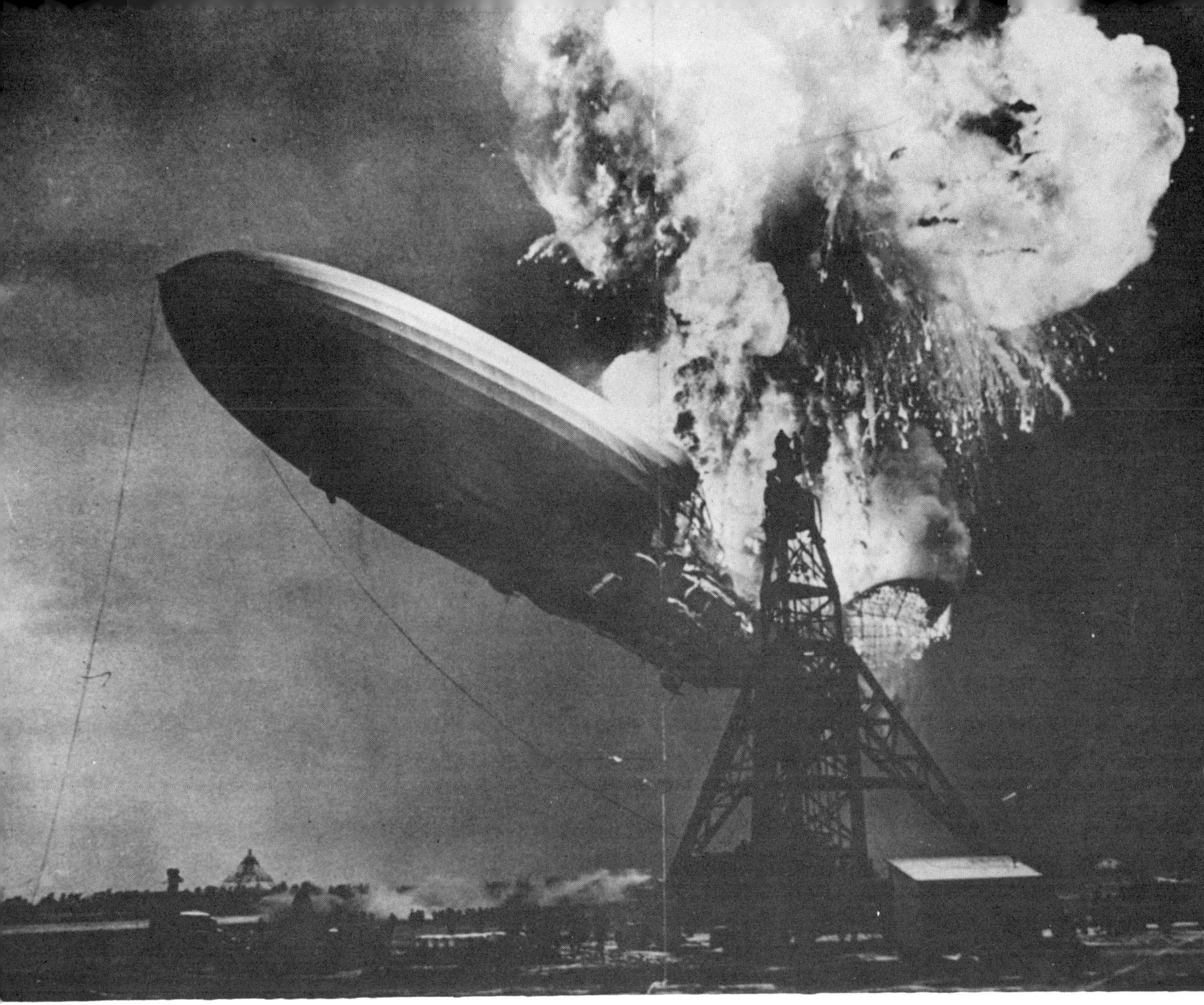

the United States, Brazil, and Japan. But the *Hinden-burg* crashed and burned out when landing at Lake-hurst, U.S.A., in May 1937; and any hope of building up a regular postal service by airship was lost in the flames.

Until about 1870 the work of the Post Office in acting as messenger had been confined to letters, post-cards and parcels. But it has kept abreast of invention by transmitting detailed messages in other ways—by telephone and telegraph, telex and teleprinter, com-munications satellite and contravision. These proved to be as revolutionary in their impact on communica-tions as Rowland Hill's proposals for Post Office reform in 1840.

The Hindenburg bursts into flames on landing at Lakehurst; 33 people were killed.

on zipnoð   god rpoll   copī   lucas
incipit euangelium   secundum lucam
                                         london
QUO
NIAM
aer   roð
QUIDE
monzo   cunnendo
MULTI
poopon   ƃre hiu ƺe
LISUTEORDINA
endo bprodnudon   ƺæt ƺenƺa
RENARRATIONEM

6: The Uses of Printing

Letters sent by the Post Office system were for centuries the main source of news. In the nineteenth and twentieth centuries two other forms of communication used mainly privately—the telegraph and telephone—became part of the Post Office service. For the general public the widespread distribution of knowledge and news not addressed to specific individuals was by book and newspaper.

Before the invention of printing the monasteries and universities were the seats of learning, and there all books were handwritten. Some of the most beautiful manuscripts were the work of several monks who divided the labour, every one being a specialist in a particular process—making the parchment, writing the text, decorating initial letters, illustrating, adding borders, and binding. This was a slow business, so for less important works the monks adopted the Roman system whereby one of them read out the text and the others wrote it down as he spoke.

In time, as the demand for manuscripts increased, men who were not monks were trained to do the work, and the kind of book altered too. Romantic adventure stories were popular, such as the legends of King Arthur and his knights, as well as books of medicinal recipes called *herbals,* and strange accounts of weird animals called *bestiaries.* In the fifteenth century Chaucer's *Canterbury Tales* was a great favourite. The

Opposite : A page from a Saxon manuscript of the gospels.

A fifteenth century monk copying a manuscript.

popularity of these books among the rich—the poor could not afford them—became so great that a quicker method of production had to be found.

Eventually a system of printing from wooden blocks was adopted. One drawback was that carving the letters in reverse was a slow process, so there was a tendency for more space to be given to illustrations and less to text—the woodcarver could afford to be less accurate with drawings than with letters. Once the wood blocks had been carved, a great many copies of the books were printed by inking the blocks and pressing them down on sheets of paper.

Wooden blocks had been used for printing by the Chinese at least 600 years before the method was followed in Europe. A fine example of a book printed by the wooden block method is a Buddhist scripture called the *Diamond Sutra*, produced in China in A.D. 868. Earthenware type was a later method perfected by the Chinese in the eleventh century; in this the words were made up from separate letters fastened together to form a large block of type. The *Diamond Sutra* was in the form

54

of a paper roll some 16 feet long, and it bore the inscription: "Printed on 11th May 868 by Wang Chieh for free general distribution, in order in deep reverence to perpetuate the memory of his parents."

The theory behind this system was applied in Europe by Johann Gutenberg, a goldsmith of Mainz, about 1430. He cast metal letters in a mould. He probably knew of the idea from information brought back from China by Marco Polo, the Venetian traveller. Gutenberg's skill lay in his ability to mould and shape the typefaces very precisely so that they fitted snugly together in the frame and gave a clear, even image. He had in partnership with him two other men, John Fust, also a goldsmith, and Peter Schoeffer. It was not a happy partnership, as there were many quarrels and intrigues. One of the most famous books they printed was called the Gutenberg Bible, of which there is a copy in the British Museum.

The English printer Caxton is presented to Edward IV.

The invention of printing in Europe came at a good time. There was a questioning of ancient beliefs; a "new learning" had come into being, fostered by universities and monasteries, and everywhere in Europe men were rethinking the relationship between God, Man and the Universe. Knowledge and opinions, to be found in books, were needed on which to base learning, education, argument and research. So the values of society in the fifteenth and sixteenth centuries were responsive to change, and new inventions flourished.

From Germany in 1454 the printer's skill spread to Switzerland, where a printing press was opened in 1466. Italy became a centre of high-class printing in 1467 after a French engraver, Nicolas Jenson, started a printing works in Venice. Jenson had been sent by Louis XI from Paris to learn the Gutenberg secrets, but instead of returning home he defected to Italy and set up in the printing business on his own account. Louis then sent another agent to Mainz who proved more reliable, and in 1470 printing by the new process was taking place in Paris.

England was the last of the major European countries to have the new printing process. William Caxton, an English merchant who undertook missions abroad for Margaret, sister of King Edward IV, visited Cologne and learned the printer's craft there. Subsequently he founded his own printing works at Bruges, where in 1474 the first book to be printed in English—*Recuyell of the Historyes of Troye*—was produced. He was also responsible for the first book to be printed in England, *Dictes or Sayenges of the Phylosophers*, which came off the press of Caxton's works at Westminster in 1477.

In all Caxton was responsible for producing about 100 books, including *Aesop's Fables*, *The Canterbury Tales* and popular romantic works, as well as books which he translated from the French.

Because readers were accustomed to the gothic

Working at a printing press in 1511.

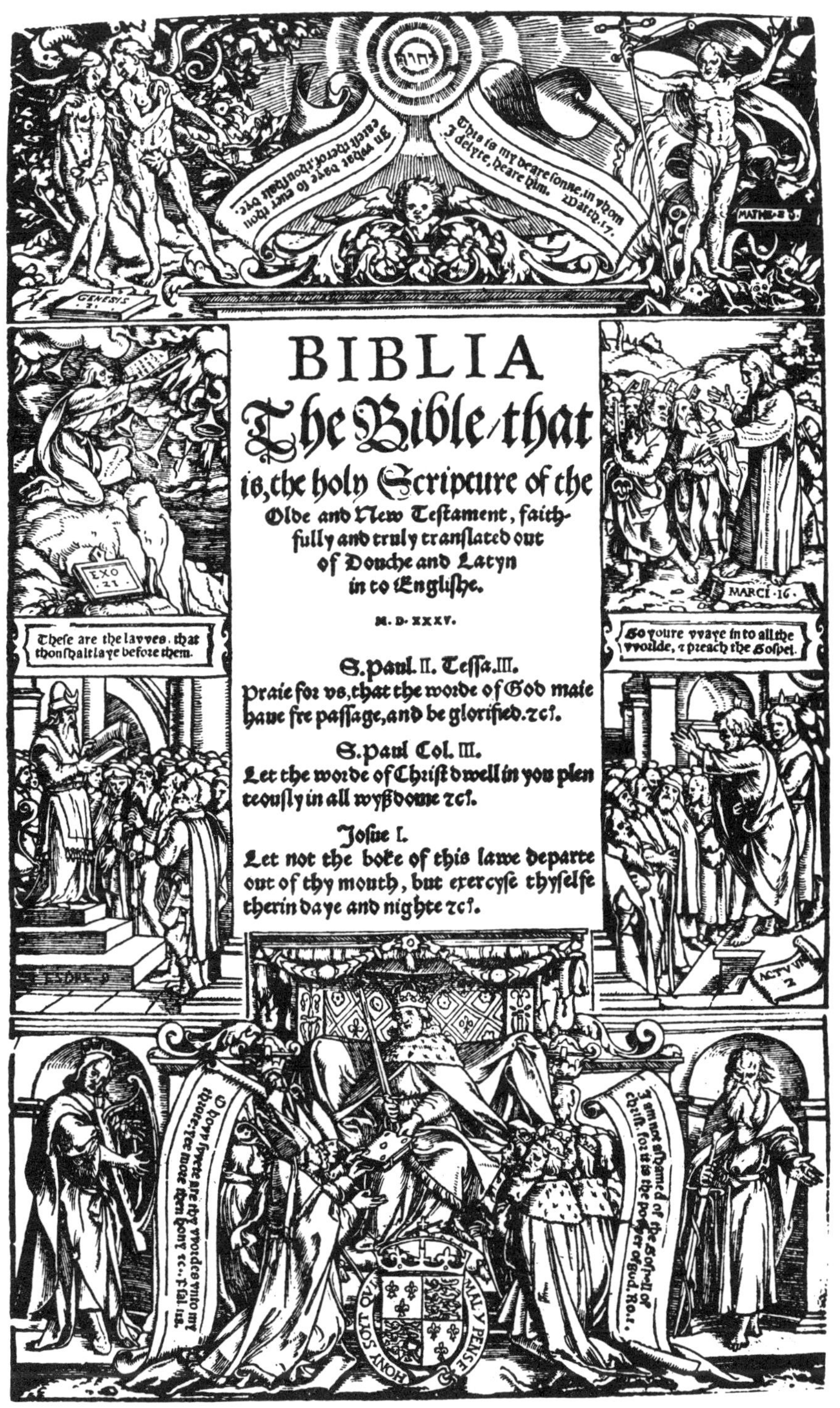

The title page of the first Bible printed in English, 1535.

Three Bloodie Murders

The firſt, committed by *Francis Cartwright* vpon *William Storre*, M
Art, Miniſter and Preacher at *Market Raiſin* in the countie of *Lincolne*.

The Second, committed by *Elizabeth Iames*, on the body of her Mayde, ii
Pariſh of *Egham* in *Surrie*: who was condemned for the ſame faĉt at Saii
Margarets hill in Southwark, the 2. of Iuly 1613. and lieth in the White Lior
till her deliuerie: diſcouered by a dombe Mayde, and a Dogge.

The Third, committed vpon a Stranger, very lately neere *High-gate* foure mil
from *London*: very ſtrangely found out by a Dogge alſo, the 2. of Iuly. 1613

handwriting used in manuscripts, the first typefaces copied this style. A change came in 1467 when in Italy a typeface was cast based on early Roman manuscripts; it was easier to read and much more attractive to the eye. This book is printed in a roman typeface called Baskerville.

Caxton not only printed books but advertised and sold them too; all printers at that time were also booksellers. However, as the industry grew larger, various specialists appeared—publishers, printers and booksellers—each concentrating on a particular aspect of the business of bringing reading material to the public.

The printing of books from the fifteenth century onwards, and of newspapers and periodicals from the sixteenth century onwards, gradually influenced the way communications were written. Before this the oral tradition was most important, changes of tone and flexibility of language being the norm, because the effect was aimed at the ear. But slowly an urbane prose style came to be the hallmark of a good writer.

The method of printing books and newspapers remained practically unchanged for four hundred years. The sheet of paper was inserted by hand under the inked typeface block, and removed when the impression had been made. At its most efficient this method turned out about 250 sheets an hour. A speeding up of the process came in the early nineteenth century with the introduction of steam; output was increased to 1,200 sheets an hour.

But if the printing process changed little in those four centuries, the content and form of the printed word altered considerably.

The Chinese are credited with having produced the first newspaper sometime during the T'ang dynasty, A.D. 618 to 906. This was a court circular, and its continuous publication under one title or another can be traced right through until the end of the *Peking Gazette* in 1912. Even earlier were the official announce-

Opposite: An illustration from a pamphlet of 1613. Then as now, papers and magazines were sold on crime and scandal.

ments of the consulship of Julius Caesar, the *Acta Diurna* that appeared from time to time as a single sheet posted in prominent public places in Rome and the provinces.

Pamphlets, each dealing with a particular subject, made their appearance in England after 1549, the first one being published by Thomas Raynalde who translated from the German *News Concernynge the General Councele Holden at Trydent*. Queen Elizabeth took advantage of the medium to deny rumours circulated by friends of Spain concerning the forthcoming invasion by the Spanish in 1588. The newspaper was called the *English Mercurie* and doubtless contained government propaganda and reassurance, one form of communication (oral gossip) being rebutted by another (printed official statements).

So the invention of printing was being put to use as a persuader of opinion. This characteristic of the printed word was to bring a swift reaction from governments in the centuries ahead who realized the threat of the new medium to their comfort and status. Pamphlets in English were printed in the Netherlands in 1620 and in England in 1621, publication being at irregular intervals. The first regular publication to appear in England was the *Weekly Newes*, issued by Nicholas Bourne and Thomas Archer in May 1622. More followed in the next decade, all exhibiting a critical attitude towards government. The power of the press was recognized in 1632 when all such news sheets and pamphlets were suppressed by government order. The Spanish ambassador had protested that information published concerning the House of Austria was highly inaccurate. So effective was the ban that for six years no news sheet appeared. The one that was allowed, under patent, to circulate in 1638 had to confine itself to foreign news.

The Star Chamber, the court which enforced the ban, was abolished in 1641, enabling the press to voice critical opinions once again. During the Civil War both

the Royalists and the Parliamentarians produced newspapers to present news and propaganda for their respective causes. *Diurnal Occurrences* was the voice of the Parliamentary party; it came out as a weekly in January 1642. A second publication, *A Perfect Diurnal of the Passages in Parliament*, also a weekly, appeared a year later, and two others followed. The Royalists produced *Mercurius Aulicus, a Diurnal Communicating the Intelligence and Affaires of the Court to the Rest of the Kingdome*, in January 1643 at Oxford, and others loyal to the King's cause later made their appearance.

While the Civil War was being fought neither side had the power to enforce restrictions. As soon as Cromwell's party won, it passed an Act of Parliament in October 1649 suppressing the independent press and permitting only official publications to appear. John Milton, the poet, was editor of one of these, *Mercurius Politicus*, for about a year.

Printing in the seventeenth century. The press is bigger and more elaborate than a hundred years before.

After the return of King Charles II in 1660 the press enjoyed a brief period of freedom. Then, seeking to stop Roundhead and Puritan criticism, the Government in 1663 passed the Licensing Act which allowed only licensed publications—those approved by the government—to be published.

The Court transferred to Oxford in 1665 to escape the plague raging in London, and here an official newspaper, the *Oxford Gazette*, was started—a timid, subservient publication. On the Court's return to London the title was altered to *London Gazette* and it remains to this day the official twice-weekly news sheet.

Many newspapers ceased to exist as a result of the Act. The number of printers in the whole of the country (they mostly worked in London) was reduced to 20. But some news still circulated. Handwritten letters became a general means of sending political information from London to the provinces, where they were circulated by the recipients. When William of Orange landed at Torbay there was no printer in the whole of the West Country who could print the new King's manifesto. Under the more tolerant atmosphere of William's reign the Licensing Act was allowed to expire in 1695, but editors, writers and printers could still be prosecuted for sedition, libel and contempt of court—a subtler method of censorship—and Parliamentary proceedings could not be reported.

Although the threat of prosecution was always present, a number of journals appeared. New publications did not start only in London; publishers found they could make money by printing local newspapers. The *Worcester Post Man* appeared in 1690, the *Edinburgh Gazette* in 1699, and the first daily newspaper, the *Daily Courant* in 1702.

7: The Growth of the Press

This growth of the provincial press was one development of the eighteenth century; another was the gradual division into publications of news and of comment. The latter took the form of periodicals, such as the *Review* started by Daniel Defoe in 1704, the *Tatler* started by Richard Steele in 1709 and the *Spectator*, started by Steele and Joseph Addison in 1711. The *Spectator* has kept going until today, with a short break, and the *Tatler* is still with us but is no longer the serious and influential journal it once was.

A determined effort by the Government to stop the flow of critical comment came with the passing of the Newspaper Stamp Act in 1712, which imposed a tax on every newspaper sold. The tax was steadily increased in the years that followed.

The effect was the opposite to that intended. Certainly circulations fell, but a greater interest was evinced in politics than ever before. Normally the reading of a newspaper is a solitary pursuit, but the tax made it a communal affair.

In London the coffee houses—of which there were about 500—were much frequented by politicians, lawyers, merchants, writers and socialites. To encourage custom the coffee house owners began to provide daily and weekly newspapers and periodicals. These were read and discussed at the tables.

The influence of the press increased, and many

Evil rewarded, innocence oppressed: a satirical anti-government cartoon of the 1770's.

illegal news sheets and pamphlets appeared, printed in secret and paying no tax. They contained far more scurrilous attacks on authority than those printed before the Stamp Act came into force.

The newspapers that paid the tax had a struggle to survive; throughout the eighteenth century new publications started up and collapsed, yet the total number of papers sold gradually increased as the interest in politics intensified. In 1753 more than seven million newspapers were sold, in 1760 the number had risen to more than nine million and by 1767 it reached eleven million. And this was among the middle and upper classes only; the mass of the public could not read.

Part of this intense interest in politics arose out of the repressive measures aimed at newspapers. No Parliamentary proceedings could be reported; this in itself was an encouragement to journalists to defy the ban. And the massive corruption in political life was always a target for attack.

What had become clear to editors in the early years of newspaper history was that criticism sells better than approval. Say what a wonderful job the government is doing and your readers will quickly become bored; criticise the government and the harder the criticism the more the readers will like it. "Print the news and raise hell!" said Wilbur Storey of the *Chicago Times* three centuries later, having come to the same conclusion.

Repression was not the only weapon used by the politicians. Various methods of persuasion were also tried. During his administration in the first half of the eighteenth century Sir Robert Walpole spent £50,000 in bribes to journalists to get them to print material favourable to him. But not all journalists could be bought, particularly those of the opposition party who were always seeking ways of reporting Parliamentary proceedings. Spurred on by the demand for news they gained access to Parliament in various ways. Once inside they took no notes as this would make them conspicuous, but memorized all they could and wrote it down from memory later.

Why did successive administrations seek to conceal their actions from the country? Many Tory politicians in the mid-eighteenth century were guided by self-interest. That self-interest would have been only too clearly exposed had speeches been published and light shed on the rampant abuses of power that were commonplace at that time. A periodical called the *North Briton* edited by John Wilkes (1725–1797), M.P. for Aylesbury, was chiefly instrumental in winning the right of the press to report Parliamentary affairs.

Wilkes was no angel. He had paid £7,000 for his Parliamentary seat and he was a member of the Hell-Fire Club whose doings scandalized even corrupt eighteenth century Britain. He was not passionately concerned about the freedom of the press. But, like the Whig party which he supported, he was eager to expose the schemes of King George III to restore the

Another use of printing: a card put out by a merchant to advertise his trade.

The reforming John Wilkes.

power of the throne by controlling Parliament through bribery and the purchase of Parliamentary seats. The Whigs had often used the same methods to control Parliament during Whig administrations.

What Wilkes hit upon was a new form of political pressure, created by rousing public opinion against the King through mass meetings held all over the country. The majority of those attending could not read, and so were badly informed about political matters. Frequently the emotions stirred were so great that riots occurred. The campaign lasted some 10 years during which Wilkes was at various times a Member of Parliament, a sheriff of London and its Lord Mayor. This did not shield him from being prosecuted, fined and imprisoned. But so successful was he in getting the public behind him that by the end of the decade many of the reforms he advocated were grudgingly accepted by the people opposed to him. This episode in history demonstrates how publicity and persistence are essential if attitudes are to be changed.

In the course of the campaign many bizarre, violent and tragic incidents occurred. In the end the freedom of the press to print Parliamentary reports was not heralded by a dramatic Act of Parliament; instead it crept in by default. The last prosecution for reporting Parliamentary affairs took place in 1771; afterwards Parliament finally and with great reluctance declined to prosecute further those journalists who persisted in publishing reports of its proceedings. More important to Wilkes and his friends was the fact that George III had been defeated in his efforts to gain control of Parliament.

1785 saw the launching of the *Daily Universal Register*. It changed its name a few years later to *The Times*, and under that title developed into one of the world's greatest newspapers. Its reputation was built up partly on the excellence of its news service—in its early days it was first with the news of the French Revolution and first with a report on Trafalgar and the death of Nelson—and partly on the range of its reporting, for it was the first British newspaper to publish full reports of Parliamentary debates. Not unexpectedly, so great was the interest in politics, the emphasis given by newspapers to Parliamentary affairs was a major factor in its success. In time it became a considerable political force.

Having helped to quash King George III's ambition to control Parliament, the press turned its attention to Parliamentary reform. Parliamentary seats, which could be bought to bolster up the strength of the Government, did not reflect the distribution of population in the country; many M.P.s represented a handful of people while some large towns had no M.P. at all.

The majority of M.P.s benefitted from the existing unjust system and so resented the efforts of newspaper editors and certain Radical politicians to alter it. Furthermore they were convinced that to extend the voting powers of the public by Parliamentary reform would encourage revolutionary movements, as in the French Revolution and the American War of Independence. So the Government labelled as seditious anything that was printed in support of wider franchise and the reallocation of Parliamentary seats.

Eighteenth century printing.

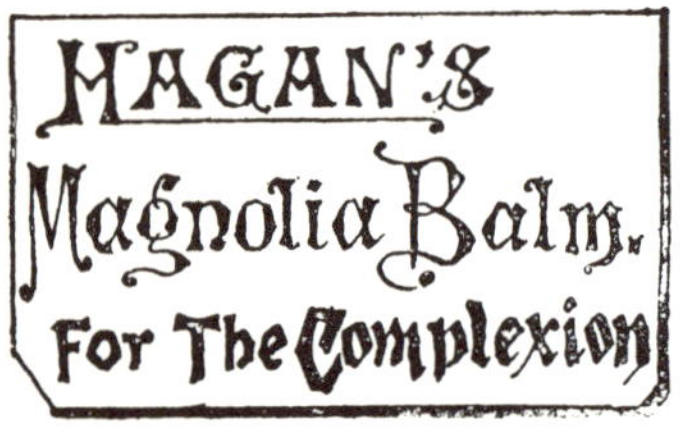

William Cobbett (1763–1835), a skilful pamphleteer and editor of the *Weekly Register,* was heavily fined and sent to prison for two years when he reported the flogging of British soldiers who had asked for arrears of pay. John Walter, founder-editor of *The Times,* also found himself in prison for defying the Government. They were not alone. The regular increases in Stamp Duty payable on newspapers, aimed at lessening their circulations and their influence, had spawned hundreds of unstamped periodicals whose editors and printers were constantly being prosecuted. And the newspaper tax was extended to periodicals of every sort and to books.

The demand for reform was strengthened by the abysmal poverty of the working classes in the industrial depression after the Napoleonic Wars. Britain seemed on the brink of revolution. Hungry mobs seized Bristol and burnt down Nottingham Castle. Partly out of fear the Reform Bill of 1832 was passed.

After this tension lessened, and some of the distrust with which the press was viewed by authority was removed. Lord Lytton persuaded Parliament in 1835 to reduce Stamp Duty from 4d to 1d.

Newspaper circulations started to rise, for the reduced tax brought the cost of a newspaper within the reach of many thousands of the literate public. In 1836 the number of newspapers sold when the tax was reduced totalled 39 million. By 1854, when Stamp Duty was abolished, the number had soared to 122 million.

The Times was well equipped to take advantage of the situation. In 1814 John Walter junior, son of the founder, had visited printing works and equipment manufacturers in Germany and had bought two steam-operated presses. They were designed so that the type moved forwards and backwards under an inking cylinder, enabling 1,200 sheets to be printed every hour instead of 250 per hour by the hand-operated method. Circulation increased to 5,000 copies of a four-page newspaper. By 1850 a 12-page paper was selling 40,000 copies a day.

The paper's reports came to be relied upon not only by individual readers but also by governments and the civil service. This gave *The Times* an influence never before achieved by any newspaper or periodical. A typical example is to be found in the reports sent from the Crimea by William Russell between 1854 and 1856. This war correspondent exposed the stupidity of much military thinking, and the appalling conditions at the base hospital at Scutari which caused additional suffering to the ill and wounded. The Government was forced to act, and Florence Nightingale and her band of helpers were permitted to go to the Crimea to establish an efficient nursing service. Communication by newspaper was thus responsible for the creation of the modern nursing profession.

At the beginning of the nineteenth century the bulk of the readership of newspapers and periodicals were middle and upper class, since, on the whole, only they knew how to read. They also had some control over Parliament because of their votes. Gradually, as the century passed, the lower classes gained in influence through the Reform Bill of 1832, the Municipal Reform Bill of 1835, the Reform Bills of 1867 and 1884 and the Local Government Act of 1888.

The need of the new voters for information offered the opportunity for newspapers to widen their appeal. The number of provincial papers grew. The *Manchester Guardian* (now the *Guardian*), launched as a Liberal weekly in 1821, became a daily penny newspaper in 1857. Later, under the editorship of C. P. Scott from 1872 to 1929, it achieved national prestige. In the nineteen-sixties it became a national paper printed in both London and Manchester.

The growing network of railways gave the London papers the chance to reach new readers in the provinces. But readership could not be greatly extended until the mass of the people were able to read.

Newspapers in the 1880's were filled with advertisements like these, appealing especially to women.

LADIES PLAYING LAWN TENNIS,
Yachting, Riding, Driving, Boating, and all exposed to the hot sun and dust, will find a most cooling and refreshing Wash for the face, hands, and arms in

ROWLANDS' KALYDOR,

HOE & Cº
UNITED STATES

The *Daily Telegraph*'s printing
machine of 1860.

There was a strong feeling in the nineteenth century among those in power that the working classes could not be trusted; and the middle and upper classes did not on the whole respond enthusiastically to demands made by some radicals that education be extended to the working classes. Eventually a low level of rudimentary education was provided—no more than tuition in the "three' Rs"—and in 1870 Forster's Education Act established a system of State elementary education. Further legislation in 1876, 1891 and 1902 expanded its scope and organization.

Just as the press had earlier responded to the growing interest in politics, it now recognized that the education of the masses provided it with a vast potential readership. Newspapers were making profits. Consequently the newspaper industry attracted business men who saw opportunities for development and had the capital to seize their chances.

First on the scene were Alfred and Harold Harmsworth, who launched the *Daily Mail* in 1896. Whereas *The Times* cost threepence (1¼p.), the price of the *Mail* was fixed at a halfpenny (¼p.) to attract the new reading public. Its style was quite new to Britain. It took for its model American sensational newspapers that had news splashed on the front page (the "serious" newspapers, *The Times* and *Daily Telegraph*, had only advertisements on the front page in those days) and many short news items, chosen for their sensational value, together with gossip and sport.

The *Mail* also took note of the popularity of the Sunday newspaper, *News of the World,* founded in 1843, which specialized, then as now, in court cases, sex, divorce and crime, and whose circulation rose to over a million by 1900, outstripping the more serious *Observer* (founded 1791) and the *Sunday Times* (founded 1822).

There were no long and serious reports on which *The Times* had built its reputation. Often the news was inaccurate, and on one occasion a report (about the

Boxer expedition in 1900) was a complete fabrication. But the working classes loved this lively new paper and in four years the *Mail's* circulation rose to a million copies. Other similar newspapers appeared—the *Daily Express*, the *Daily Mirror*, the *Daily Sketch*. The *Daily News*, founded in 1846 with Charles Dickens as editor, was forced to become more popular in its appeal.

There were other reasons for the success of the popular press. Technical improvements made the printing process faster and new inventions enabled news to be swiftly transmitted.

The work of scientists like Charles Wheatstone in England and Samuel Morse in America made a system of communication, based on transmitting electrical impulses along a cable, commercially viable in the mid-nineteenth century. For the press, this was exploited by Julius Reuter who set up a news-agency service that was destined to become world famous.

The telegraph transmitted messages which needed decoding. A more astonishing invention followed—that of the telephone which transmitted the human voice. Two Americans, Dr. C. C. Page and Alexander Graham Bell, were responsible for the basic research, although the credit for the finished invention is usually given to Bell. A visit to London by Bell in 1878 led to the installation of a telephone link between the House of Commons and Fleet Street.

The steam-operated printing press had been brought into use by all the national newspapers following its adoption by *The Times* in 1814. The next big step forward in the mass production of newspapers came in 1863 when William Bullock in America perfected a rotary press. The principle underlying Bullock's invention was that of a continuous printing process on a large roll of paper, achieved by having the type and the ink mounted on rotating cylinders. The earlier presses printed a single sheet at a time, but the rotary press printed continuously, the newsprint being subsequently cut into sheets and folded. The advantages

Selling newspapers to the first class compartment, in about 1905.

C*

gained by using Bullock's machine were increased in 1875 by a process that made a kind of paper called newsprint from cheap wood pulp.

Yet another contribution to instant news was the automatic typesetting machine patented by the American Ottmar Mergenthaler in 1885. Formerly all typesetting had been done by hand; Mergenthaler's invention enabled type to be set five times as fast.

The second half of the nineteenth century was one of ferment for the newspaper industry. It was like watching a mad scientist in a film, adding one ingredient to another in a flask, seeing the mixture begin to boil and bubble as it gave off a dense and penetrating vapour.

The reporting of Parliamentary affairs, together with the increased franchise, led to a still greater interest being taken in central and local government. The growth of literacy provided a mass market for newspapers that specialized in sensational journalism. To meet the demand production was increased by the use of new printing processes. Competition between rival newspapers hastened the adoption of the telegraph and telephone for transmitting news, and the railways provided the means of sending the printed word overnight to all parts of the country.

Readers felt a greater involvement with events. This feeling had been lacking in the early years of the century, when much provincial news often took several days to reach the public and foreign news considerably longer—details of the Battle of Trafalgar in 1805 did not reach London until 16 days after it had taken place! This immediacy which the press provided boosted the appeal of newspapers and heralded the golden years of journalism.

The poster announcing the news of Trafalgar in London. The battle had taken place on 21 October, but England did not hear of it for 16 days.

8: Telegraph and Telephone

Electricity was the power behind the new inventions. If one man can be said to be responsible for the major step leading to the telegraph and telephone, it was Otto von Guericke of Magdeburg in Germany, who in 1650 produced an electric charge in a ball of sulphur by rubbing it with his hands. This was the first electricity-making process. After this many scientists tried to perfect apparatus that would send electricity along a conductor from one place to another. In Britain Sir William Watson did this in 1747. The brilliance of men like him lay not in discovering electricity—that had already been done—but in its efficient application. They were striving to construct apparatus that could be depended upon to work not just once or twice but for a considerable time.

Sir Humphry Davy and Francis Ronalds in Britain, Baron von Schilling in Russia and Germany, Alessandro Volta in Italy, André Marie Ampère in France, Hans Christian Oersted in Denmark and Joseph Henry and Samuel Morse in America were some of the many scientists who contributed in the first half of the nineteenth century to the knowledge of electricity. Oersted specialized in electro-magnetism; it was he who discovered that an electric current could deflect a magnetic needle. Ampère found out more about this. Schilling went further and made a five-needle telegraph that he demonstrated in Bonn in

1835. It was seen by William Fothergill Cooke, an Englishman working in Germany.

When Cooke returned to London he contacted Professor Charles Wheatstone of London University. Together they developed the Schilling idea and demonstrated it in London in 1837. A current of electricity was sent along a five-wire cable, each strand being attached to a needle at the receiving station. These five needles were inside a diamond-shaped box together with a panel on which was set out the letters of the alphabet and numbers from 0 to 9.

When the operator pressed a button alongside the letter he wished to transmit, two of the needles deflected in the panel at the receiving station, their convergence indicating the letter intended. The electricity was kept flowing in the despatch station by hand-cranking a generator.

When Cooke and Wheatstone demonstrated their

Cooke's and Wheatstone's two-needle telegraph of 1846.

apparatus the railways were being developed rapidly, and any inventions that could improve performance were welcomed. The directors of the London and North Western Railway saw the electric-needle telegraph as a reliable means of notifying the movements of trains between one station and another, and they employed Cooke and Wheatstone. The world's first commercial telegraph line was laid in 1837 between Euston and Camden. Two years later the Great Western Railway installed the system along the 19-mile stretch between Paddington and West Drayton, near Slough. By that time skilled telegraph operators could send and decode about 20 words a minute.

Businessmen invested capital in private companies to extend the use of the needle-telegraph. Cooke and Wheatstone helped to form the Electric Telegraph Company that laid some 4,000 miles of cable between 1846 and 1852. Members of the public could send

A telegraphic instrument invented by Wheatstone in 1840. One dial was for transmitting and one for receiving. One of these instruments was still being used by the Post Office in North Wales in 1950.

messages, the rate varying according to the distance; London to Birmingham cost 4d ($1\frac{1}{2}$p.) a word, London to Glasgow 6d ($2\frac{1}{2}$p.). The City of London had its own telegraph office in Lothbury Street, E.C.1, to make dealings easier in stocks and shares and the money market.

Cooke and Wheatstone had been able to improve on their original five-needle system before they launched the company. They produced a single-needle instrument in 1845 and established a code that made it unnecessary to spell out every word letter by letter. Eventually, however, they found it speedier to adopt the Morse buzzer telegraph system in use in America. On some stretches of railway line, however, the original Cooke-Wheatstone code remained in use right into the twentieth century.

Although the electric telegraph had been theoretically possible for many years, and scientists in various countries had been trying to develop a reliable instrument, the solution came suddenly to an American portrait painter, Samuel Finley Breese Morse, in 1832. He was an artist without any scientific background or knowledge—and so his emergence as a scientist at the age of 40 shows that many of us may have aptitudes of which we are not aware.

In 1826 Morse was the President of the National Academy of Design and had built up a modest reputation as an artist. In 1832 he returned from a trip to Europe where he had been studying art. On board he saw a demonstration of electro-magnetism. A soft piece of iron became a magnet when an electric current was passed through a length of wire coiled around it. This magnetic quality was strong enough to cause another piece of metal to adhere to the soft iron core, and to fall away when the current was stopped. The passenger performing the experiment was repeating what he had seen Professor Ampère do at a demonstration of electro-magnetism in Paris.

Morse immediately realized the implications of

Samuel Finley Breese Morse, the American inventor.

The Morse telegraph wire stretches across the American continent.

what he had seen—that the contact and break between magnet and armature could be used in the form of a signal. Had he been aware of the considerable amount of work currently being done on these lines Morse might not have turned scientist. However, believing he was on to something quite new, he set up a workshop and began to experiment in his spare time. Money came from his salary as Professor of the Literature of the Arts of Design at New York University, and by 1835 he had constructed a fairly reliable but amateurish instrument. It was only then that he was told of the similar work done by his countryman Joseph Henry. One of his students, Alfred Vail, whose father owned a prosperous ironworks, provided materials and money to build a demonstration model.

This was shown to the public in the Hall of New York University in 1837, messages being sent from one end of the Hall to the other along a cable. At the despatch station a tapper device operated to spell out

FARADAY

The launching of the *Faraday*, telegraph cable-laying ship, in 1874. The beginning of the undersea cable system, which has since stretched all over the world, dramatically changed the pattern of communications. Far-off countries suddenly seemed much nearer.

the words in a series of dots and dashes. At the receiving station at the other end of the Hall a buzzer announced the message. The code combination of dots and dashes had been perfected by Morse, and he had taken the trouble to 'streamline' it, for example by first finding out what letters were most in use (E and T) and giving these the single dot or dash symbol. This code, which bears its inventor's name, is now in use, slightly altered, all over the world.

Getting permission to put up a telegraph line was a slow business, but meanwhile Morse was not idle. He continued to experiment and, by laying a cable from Battery Park, Manhattan, to Governor's Island, New York, proved that underwater transmission was possible. Eventually, in 1843, a Bill was passed authorizing $30,000 to be spent on installing the telegraph along a 40-mile stretch between Washington and Baltimore. The following year the project was completed. Morse sent the first message along the wire, "What hath God wrought!"—the choice of words being indicative of the religious beliefs of the time.

With the Morse system gradually spreading its network of wires over the eastern side of North America and parts of Europe, and the Cooke–Wheatstone system spreading over Britain and being adopted by the Post Office and the Army as well as the railways, it was inevitable that efforts should be made to link the two.

Several undersea cables were laid, the most important being Britain to France (1853), Britain to Ireland (1854) and Ireland to Newfoundland (1858). The last occasion was marked by the exchange of official platitudes between Queen Victoria and the President of the United States, but two months after this conversation the cable broke; it was not until 1866, eight years later, that a replacement was laid successfully.

After the Morse system of transmitting messages had been adopted by Britain for inter-continental messages, Wheatstone still further improved the telegraph service.

The telegraph office in the City of London in 1871. It has changed a good deal since then!

In 1867 he perfected a method of punching the message in Morse code on a paper tape. The tape passed through the transmitter and the holes punched in it were transformed into electrical impulses. At the receiving end an instrument printed out the dots and dashes on another tape and these were read by the operator. Between 200 and 300 words a minute could be transmitted in this way.

One example of the use of the electric-needle telegraph in everyday life caught the imagination of the public in 1845. On 1st January of that year John Tawell committed a murder by poisoning at Salthill, near Slough. Suspicion fell on him, and he was seen to board the 7.42 p.m. train from Slough to London, wearing a brown greatcoat reaching almost to his feet. In the telegraph office at Paddington station a message came through from Slough describing Tawell.

The assassination of President
Lincoln. Reuter's was the first
with the news back to
England.

Police were waiting when the train arrived in London
and they picked out Tawell from the description. He
was followed to a public house near London Bridge
and arrested. At the trial he was found guilty and
hanged. The part played by the telegraph in this
affair gave rise to a catchphrase about telegraph wires
that were called "the cords that hanged John Tawell."

Telegraphy helped newspapers to improve the
service they offered to their readers; but it was an
outsider who demonstrated how speedily news could
be obtained. Julius Reuter, a German who later became
a naturalized Englishman, had a flair for improvising
ways of transmitting news using both new and trusted
methods. He was in Europe when telegraph cables
were being laid in many of the principal countries.
The Belgian cable ended at Brussels, the German cable
at Aachen. News between these two cities went by

train. Reuter established a pigeon service which beat the train by seven hours.

He moved to London when the Channel undersea cable was laid, opened a telegraph office near the Stock Exchange, and in a few years was supplying newspapers with news from abroad.

He was never satisfied with what looked like the swiftest possible means of communication. News despatches from the American Civil War reached Britain by mailboat, landing at Queenstown, Ireland. They were then taken 20 miles to Cork for telegraphing to London. Reuter set up his own telegraph wire from Crookshaven, on the westernmost point of Ireland, to Cork. Then he arranged for his despatches from America to be dropped overboard from the mailboats as they rounded Crookshaven point where a launch was waiting to pick them up. The mailboats still had several hours to go before reaching Queenstown. In this time Reuter's men had telegraphed the war news to Cork and thence onward to London. Sometimes, when conditions were bad, the Reuter service was almost twenty-four hours faster than the normal service via Queenstown. The news of Abraham Lincoln's assassination was another triumph for Reuter's service. A Reuter correspondent witnessed the shooting in the theatre and telegraphed the news to New York, where it was rushed to the mailboat quay. The once-weekly boat had just sailed. Reuter's man hired a fast small boat, chased out to sea after the mailboat and got his despatch aboard. It was dropped off at Crookshaven to be picked up by Reuter's launch.

Reuter's strength lay not only in his emphasis on speed but also on independence and integrity of reporting. Because Reuter reports were trustworthy, and never sensational when there was no sensation to report, the very name Reuter came to be accepted on a press report as a guarantee of authenticity. The success of the agency enabled it to expand all over the world, and it remains the foremost news agency today.

Alexander Graham Bell in
1900.

One immediate effect of the new inter-continental communication system was to help stabilize commerce by lessening the risks taken by businessmen engaged in world trade. Before the era of rapid communications, markets could change very considerably in "long-distance" trades, between the placing of orders and the delivery of goods. Crop failures, war, insurrection and drought affected the ability of foreign customers to pay for goods. The telegraph and later the telephone enabled merchants to gain knowledge of current conditions overseas which could prevent heavy losses or even bankruptcy.

The development of a workable electro-magnetic telegraph was firmly based on the work of a number of scientists. The development of the telephone followed a similar pattern. Yet it was Alexander Graham Bell who eventually received the accolade as the instrument's inventor.

Bell, like Morse, was not a scientist by profession. He was primarily interested in human speech. His early life contains several anecdotes illustrating this interest. He tried to teach his Skye terrier to talk. He is reported to have made a replica of a human head that, with the aid of a pair of bellows, emitted a sound resembling "Mamma!"

While studying at Edinburgh University he came across a telephone made in 1861 by the German scientist Johann Reiss. This was an elementary instrument with a stretched membrane that vibrated to a particular musical pitch. The vibrating membrane made and broke contact with an electric circuit and musical sounds were given out by the receiving instrument. A tune of a song could be recognized but not the words.

Bell's two brothers died of tuberculosis and in 1870 the rest of the family emigrated to Canada to escape the risk of catching the disease. Bell, who was a teacher of the deaf, later moved to Boston, Massachusetts, where he set up a school to train teachers of the deaf.

In June 1875 he succeeded in transmitting a human voice from one room in the house to another. There was not enough power to extend the range until Bell used an invention of Edison's, a variable-contact carbon transmitter. Seeing the commercial possibilities of the instrument Bell took out a patent for it in March 1876, demonstrated it at the Philadelphia Centennial Exhibition in June, and formed the Bell Telephone Company in 1877.

When Bell was on his honeymoon in Britain in 1878 (he married a deaf mute who was one of his pupils) he arranged several demonstrations of the telephone.

He had a cable laid from the gallery of the House of Commons to Fleet Street, enabling the progress of a Parliamentary debate to be dictated to a newspaper shorthand writer.

Bell's first telephone, 1876.

BELL'S TELEPHONE.

THE ELECTRIC TELEPHONE COMPANY,

115, CANNON STREET, E.C.,

IS NOW READY TO EXECUTE ORDERS

FOR THE

Rental or Purchase of Telephones.

ESTIMATES

ARE ALSO FURNISHED

For the CONSTRUCTION of TELEPHONIC LINES.

Local Companies will be established in all the principal Towns of the United Kingdom.

The public is hereby cautioned against purchasing or using cheap imitations of Bell's Telephone, as they are infringements of Professor Bell's Patent. All makers, sellers, or users of such spurious instruments will be prosecuted to the full extent of the law.

A second demonstration, for Queen Victoria at Osborne House, Isle of Wight, held on 14th January, turned out to be no simple display of speaking from one room to another. Wires had been laid to Osborne Cottage nearby, where a singer rendered *Kathleen Mavourneen, Coming Thro' the Rye* and the epilogue to *As You Like It*. Contact had been made, too, with Southampton and London. From the capital, 80 miles away, an organ recital was clearly heard. The demonstration so captivated the Royal party that it went on until midnight.

The Queen's earlier enthusiasm for railway travel had set the seal of approval on it. Now her approval of the telephone gave its sponsors the impetus they needed to make it a commercial success in Britain.

The Edison Company, which was already selling telephones publicly in New York, now started a telephone service in London. A telephone exchange was opened linking, at first, seven or eight subscribers, the switchboard being manually operated and the operator being called by turning a handle on the set. Five years later the exchange in East India Avenue had 271 subscribers and 46 trunk and other direct lines. About 2,400 calls a day were handled by the lady operators. Special services were available. All the major London theatres and concert halls were linked to the exchanges and subscribers for a fee could be connected to hear the performance in progress.

The British Post Office, like its American counterpart, saw the telegraph and telephone as threats to its business. But officials watched the progress of the new system with keen interest. And in time—acting on the principle "if you can't beat them, join them"—the Post Office started its own telephone service. The various small private telephone companies, which had been competing against each other, united in 1889 to form the National Telephone Company. But when the undersea link between Britain and France was established in 1891, the Post Office persuaded Parliament

Bell's advertisement in the newspapers when he arrived in England in 1878. Queen Victoria was much impressed with his invention.

Bell makes the first phone call from New York to Chicago—a long way in those days—in 1892.

that for security and monetary reasons the Government should run both this important international service and the internal trunk lines linking one city with another. In 1912 all local telephone lines were brought under Post Office control. Thus the State acquired the power to monitor certain forms of communication between individuals, a power which has been increasingly exercised.

9: Sending Messages Through the Air

The arrest and hanging of John Tawell in 1845 brought the electro-magnetic telegraph firmly before the general public. In 1910 the arrest, trial and hanging of Dr. Crippen did the same for a more astonishing form of communication, wireless telegraphy.

On the 16th July 1910 a warrant was issued for the arrest of Dr. Hawley Harvey Crippen and Miss Ethel le Neve on a charge of murdering Crippen's wife. The doctor had vanished from his Camden house, and the police issued a description of the two wanted persons to the newspapers.

This description was read by Captain H. G. Kendall, master of the Canadian Pacific liner *Montrose* at Antwerp, where the ship was about to sail for Canada. Two of his passengers caught his attention, a Dr. Robinson and his son. Captain Kendall first became suspicious because the son looked more like a girl than a boy. Secondly, the Doctor was growing a beard and although he was not wearing glasses, there was a red mark on the bridge of his nose, showing that he usually wore them. Obviously, the Captain thought, remembering the police description, this man has shaved off his moustache, has removed his glasses and is growing a beard as a disguise.

He bound the radio operator to secrecy and had a wireless message sent to the shore station at Poldhu in Cornwall, stating his strong suspicion that Dr. Crippen

Ethel le Neve dressed as a boy.

and Ethel le Neve were on board. The local police at Poldhu passed the information on to Scotland Yard. Immediately Chief Inspector Drew booked a berth on a fast liner shortly to leave Liverpool, the *Laurentic*, which was scheduled to reach Canada before the much slower *Montrose*. In the St. Lawrence River, Drew boarded the *Montrose*. After a brief talk with the Captain and a few minutes' observation of "Dr. Robinson and son" he arrested the two passengers. Crippen was later hanged for murder; Ethel le Neve was acquitted. At the trial the newspapers made dramatic headlines out of the part played by wireless in the case—one reporter going so far as to describe wireless as "an invisible bloodhound following the scent over the high seas!"

The theories behind wireless were first developed by James Clerk Maxwell, a Scottish physicist, who published a mathematical treatise in 1873 on the electromagnetic theory of light. The theory was that electrical phenomena in the form of waves can travel with the speed of light—186,000 miles per second. Maxwell foretold that waves generated by electrical phenomena could have wavelengths ranging from a few inches to several miles, and that men would be able to discover and make use of these longer waves which are now called radio waves.

Later investigations have validated this theory. X-rays, light rays and radio waves are exactly the same—all electro-magnetic waves—apart from differences in wavelength; and the electro-magnetic theory of light is the theoretical foundation of a whole new era of communications.

The investigations of a German scientist, Heinrich Hertz, showed—as Maxwell had predicted—that electro-magnetic waves travel at 186,000 miles per second and behave in the same way as light waves. In one experiment he demonstrated that a polished metal plate acting as a mirror reflected the waves just as it reflected light waves, showing that they both travel in straight lines. A concave metal plate concentrated them in a beam just as a concave mirror did with light. Hertz could deflect the waves with lenses and prisms made with paraffin wax or pitch.

The most crucial of Hertz's experiments took place in 1887 when he proved his contention, based on Maxwell's theory, that electro-magnetic waves (or radio waves as they later became known) could move across space. An Englishman, Ernest Rutherford, succeeded in 1895 in transmitting signals over three quarters of a mile.

The year before Rutherford's demonstration, Guglielmo Marconi, a student at Bologna University, had read of Hertz's experiment and determined to take it a stage further. Whereas Hertz had sent out a continuous flow of waves in his experiment, Marconi, by using a Morse code tapper, was able to break up the wave transmission into long and short periods, corresponding to the Morse code dash and dot. In this way he built up a message in code which announced

Marconi with his assistant.

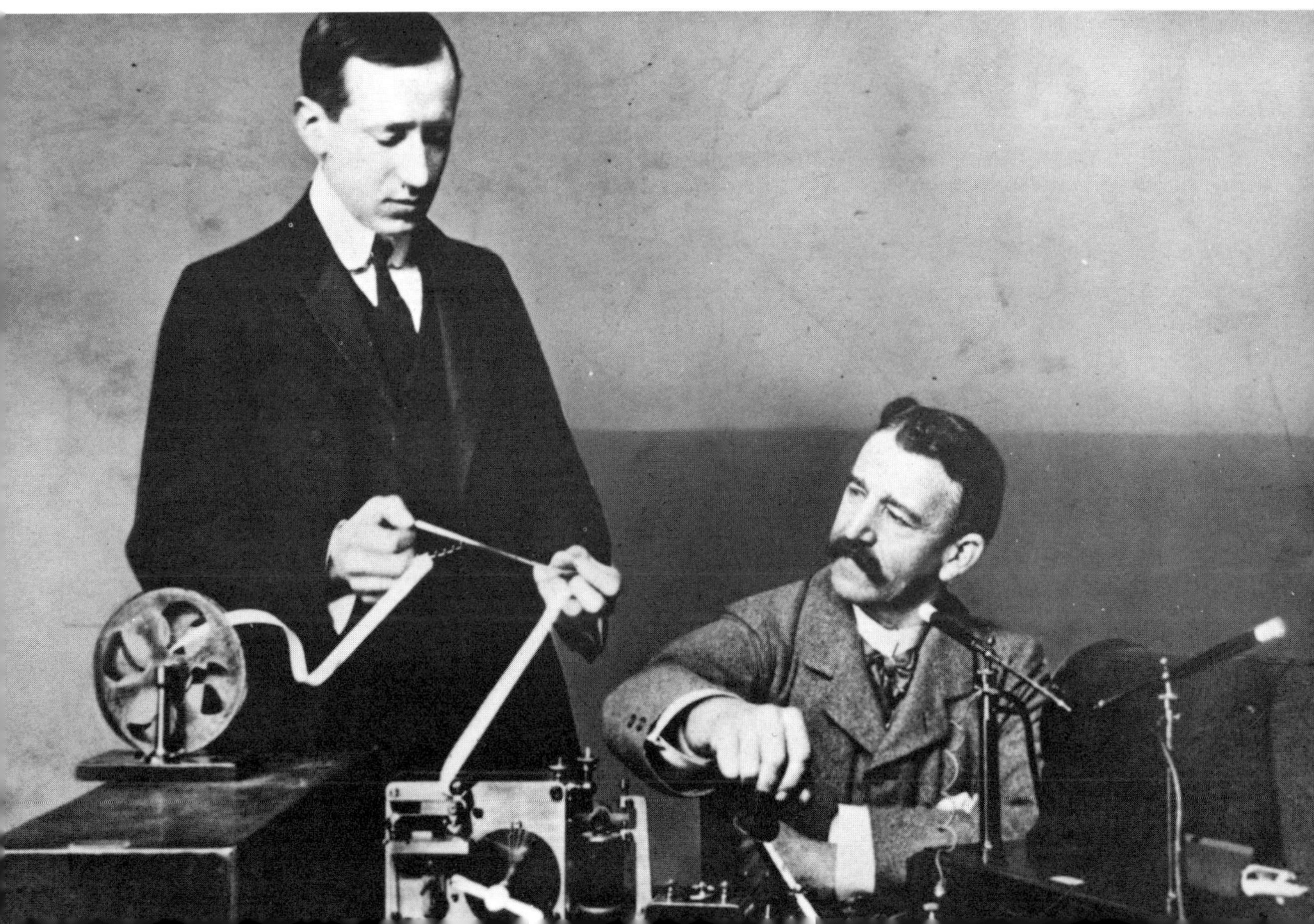

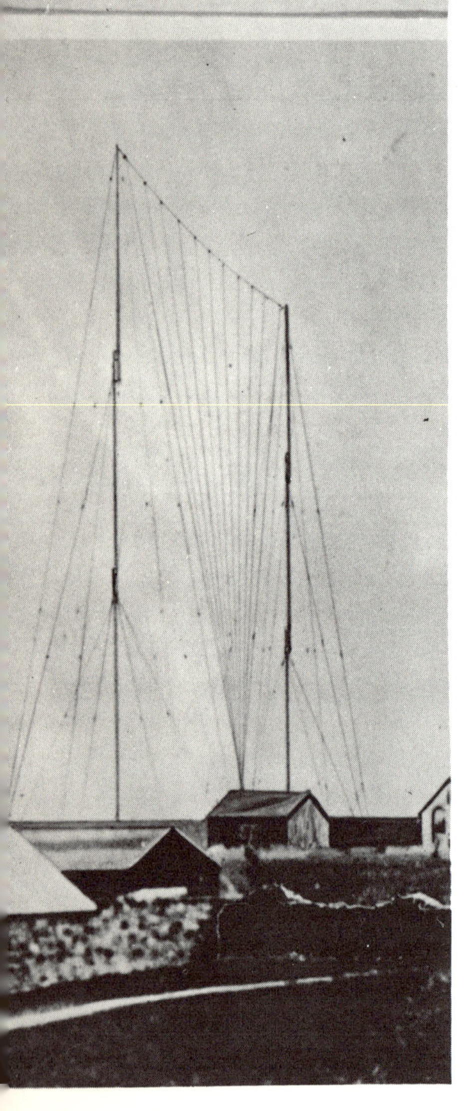
Marconi's wireless station at Poldhu, Cornwall.

itself on the broken ring 12 feet away in a series of short and long breaks in a flow of sparks.

By 1896 with better apparatus the distance had been increased to two miles. Marconi approached the Italian naval authorities and pointed out the value of the system for sending Morse code messages from ship to ship, or ship to shore, but they were not interested. He was then persuaded by his Irish-born mother to go to England where she felt he would have a better chance.

She was right. The Post Office showed its traditional willingness to investigate the performance of any invention likely to improve communications. Sir William Preece, head of its telegraph department, arranged a demonstration on the roof of the Post Office building in St. Martin's-le-Grand. Officials witnessing the demonstration were enthusiastic; Marconi's contention that wire-less telegraphy was possible had been proved to their satisfaction.

The endorsement given to his work by the Post Office was the turning point in Marconi's career. The next few years were full of activity. He formed the Marconi Wireless Telegraph Company which erected the first two wireless stations ever to be built, one at Bournemouth and the other on the Isle of Wight. He demonstrated wireless telegraphy to the Army and the Royal Navy on Salisbury Plain and proved that the system would work between ships and ships, and ships and land. In 1869 he was the first man to send instantaneous messages across the Channel without using the undersea cable.

The value of the new method of communication in real life situations was shown on several occasions. The number of ships fitted with wireless began to increase. A shipwreck with loss of life was prevented in 1899 when shore-based lifeboats were alerted by wireless telegraphy. It was used to send reports of the condition of the Prince of Wales (later Edward VII) from the royal yacht off the Isle of Wight to Queen Victoria, on

the island, when he was taken ill aboard ship. The first use of it by the press came when a ship, fitted with wireless, reported on a yacht race at Kingstown Regatta, off the Irish coast.

Marconi's greatest triumph came in 1901. The year before, the Marconi Wireless Telegraphy Company had been granted the sole right to send messages by wireless waves. He had then erected a wireless station at Poldhu, near Lands End, which he planned to use for the transmission of transatlantic messages. Three towers were built before one was made strong enough to withstand the heavy winds.

There were a number of questions about this venture to which no-one knew the answer. Would the curvature of the Earth influence the outcome of the experiment? Would wireless waves follow the Earth's curvature or would they keep on a straight line and so be lost in space? The answers would not be found until the experiment was tried. So Marconi installed his transmitting apparatus in the Poldhu tower. He gave detailed instructions to his assistants to send a special Morse signal, the three dots for S, on a day and time arranged. Then he sailed for Newfoundland.

There the winter weather was so bad that he could not build a receiving tower. Marconi decided to use a kite to lift 400 feet into the sky a wire aerial that was connected to the ground. Thirty minutes after midday

Getting ready to fly the kite in Newfoundland to receive the first transatlantic wireless signals.

95

on 12th December 1901 Marconi heard three sharp clicks in his headphones. It was repeated. The S signal sent out from Poldhu more than two thousand miles away had got through.

Obviously, he thought, the curvature of the Earth had not affected the transmission. In fact the wireless waves had not followed the Earth's curvature but had gone into space some 200 miles where they had met the ionosphere, a layer of gases that acted as a barrier. Against this barrier they bounced back into the Earth's atmosphere. Today this is known; signals are aimed at the ionosphere, and messages to the other side of the globe reach their destination by being deflected back to the Earth.

Not only does a dramatic situation make us appreciate the value of an invention, it also serves to concentrate attention on the way it is used. So it was with the sinking of the *Titanic* in 1912. This liner, the world's

SS *Titanic* on her trials at Belfast in 1912.

The *Titanic*'s last message.

largest at that time and reputed to be unsinkable, was
fitted with the most up-to-date equipment, including
a wireless transmitter and receiver. This was a great
advance, as the traditional way for ships to call for
help was by rocket or gunfire.

On 12th April on its maiden voyage from Southampton to New York the *Titanic* picked up wireless messages
from at least six other ships in mid-Atlantic, warning
of the existence of icebergs directly in the *Titanic*'s
path. Such was the confidence of the captain and
officers that they continued full steam ahead at $22\frac{1}{2}$
knots into the danger area.

Shortly before midnight an iceberg was sighted
ahead, but it was too late to avoid a collision. The
iceberg tore a gash some 100 yards in length under the
waterline of the liner.

Wireless signals were sent out, the operators first
using the old code CQD, CQD, and giving the *Titanic*'s
position, later using the newly-introduced international
distress signal SOS. Soon the belief that the ship was
unsinkable was shown to be false; the captain gave the
order to abandon ship.

Other ships in the area had heard the signals for help and had responded. The first to arrive on the scene at 4.10 a.m. was the Cunard liner *Carpathia*. But the *Titanic* had sunk nearly two hours before, at 2.20 a.m., and of its 1,319 passengers and 889 crew less than 800 survivors in lifeboats were picked up. All who had jumped overboard, hoping to keep afloat in the icy seas, were drowned.

But the *Carpathia* was not the nearest ship to the *Titanic*. Only a few miles away was the *Californian*, which had stopped because of the danger from ice. But this ship's wireless operator had switched off his apparatus shortly after 11.30 p.m. and had gone to bed. Had the *Titanic*'s signals been received the *Californian* could have reached the stricken liner in time to take off most if not all of her passengers and crew.

The *Titanic* used another method of signalling for help. When the danger of sinking became apparent, eight rockets were fired. These were seen by sailors aboard the *Californian*, and, although rocket flares are universally known to be a cry for help, the captain of the *Californian* took no action.

As a result of the *Titanic* disaster, international agreement was reached on the use of wireless at sea. A wireless operator was to be on duty all the time, day and night. To make sure that distress signals were heard for a few minutes every half-hour no ordinary messages were to be sent, and during this time operators were to listen for cries for help from other ships.

Marconi's invention had proved its worth. The British Postmaster General, Mr. Herbert Samuel, said at the time, "Those who were saved were saved through one man, Mr. Marconi." The great loss of life was due not to the invention but to man's inefficient use of it. And the indifference shown by the captain of the *Californian* to the *Titanic*'s rocket signals points the moral that, even if a communication is received, it is not effective unless acted upon.

The problem of amplifying weak currents and of

transmitting speech by wireless, and so giving wireless telegraphy and the telephone a much greater range, was solved by an American scientist, Lee de Forest. He developed further the work done on a thermionic valve by Professor Ambrose Fleming, and in 1906 produced the audion vacuum tube that could amplify, magnify or generate waves as well as detect radio signals. It could amplify speech impulses from a microphone and these were sent with wireless waves to a receiver where they were converted back again into speech.

This invention was called the jack-of-all-trades. The valve became the core of each transmitter, of each receiver and the vital link in telephonic communication over long distances. In time it led to the electrical recording and reproduction of gramophone records, talking films, photo-telegraphy and radio direction of ships and planes. It is essential to the accurate working of automatic regulators, calculating machines, computers, measuring instruments and alarms fitted with photo-electric cells. The invention was the only reliable electronic amplifier for nearly 40 years, when the modern transistor took over most of its uses. For the part he played in the development of modern communications, Lee de Forest must rank with Morse, Bell and Marconi.

Men who had learnt the elements of wireless telegraphy during the First World War swelled the number of people interested in this form of communication. Some became enthusiasts, building their own transmitters and receivers and getting in touch over the air with fellow enthusiasts. The amount of interest shown was much greater in America than in Britain; and the first broadcasting station was opened at Pittsburg in 1920. Britain followed. A broadcasting station at Chelmsford was set up in February 1922 where once-a-week programmes lasting half-an-hour were transmitted. Even so the power was only 100-watt. A second station was set up in May in London at Savoy Hill, using the call-sign 2LO. Later, the British Broad-

An early broadcast of a concert on the radio, 1923.

casting Company (later to become a Corporation) was formed by a number of radio equipment manufacturers. It was granted the sole right of broadcasting in the United Kingdom; regular nightly broadcasting began in November 1922 from London, and from Birmingham and Manchester soon afterwards.

10: Records, Cinema, Television

The history of sound recording goes back to 1857, when Leon Scott, an Irishman living in France, built a machine to record sound. It was shown as a wavy line on the smoked surface of a rotating cylinder which he called the phonautograph. Little interest was shown in this until twenty years later when an American, Thomas Edison, who had left school at the age of twelve after only three months' education, made a device which not only recorded sound but also played it back. Edison reproduced the sound of his own voice reciting *Mary Had A Little Lamb*. His machine, the phonograph, consisted of a cylinder covered in tin foil. Indentations were cut on this by a vibrating stylus attached to a diaphragm. The popularity of the phonograph grew, but it was regarded mainly as an elaborate toy. Edison did not develop it further at that time as he had so many other interests.

Several years after this first demonstration Alexander Graham Bell became interested. He enlisted the help of two other scientists, Chichester Bell and Charles Tainter, and they began experimenting in Bell's laboratory. They got the best results with a machine like Edison's, but they used wax instead of tin foil as this gave better sound reproduction. In 1885 Chichester Bell and Tainter applied for a patent and two years later formed a company to make and sell their gramophone.

Thomas Edison with a
phonograph, one of his many
inventions.

Edison returned to his experiments and found that a wax cylinder was an improvement on tin foil. He too formed his own company to sell the phonograph.

Sound reproduction was so good by this time that many famous people, including Gladstone and Robert Browning, had their voices recorded. An early musical recording was Brahms playing one of his works. But production was slow. Multi-recordings were not yet possible; to make a number of recordings at once, the artist had to speak or sing in front of several microphones. This was very slow, and the companies could barely keep pace with demand.

The problem was solved by German-born Emile Berliner, who invented the disc. He recorded sound as a wavy spiral on a flat zinc disc. It was coated with a thin layer of fat to protect it from acid treatment except where the line was etched. The acid bath then left a groove. Berliner did not want to use the etched master copy for playing, so he made a negative from it by electro-forming, and then records were moulded from the negative in a form of thermoplastic material like our present-day discs.

These records were far tougher than the wax cylinders, and were louder too. In 1894 Berliner started manufacturing. He was always on the look-out for improvements. He could see that driving the machine by a hand-crank was not very satisfactory; so his company produced a practical design for a spring-driven motor governed by friction. Competition between cylinder and disc records lasted until the end of the century, when the popularity of the disc was undisputed.

Business was good. More companies were formed both in the U.S. and in Europe.

At the beginning of the twentieth century the Odeon Company of Berlin produced discs with recordings on both sides. Other companies did the same, and later that year the Victor Company redesigned their gramophone, doing away with the big horn used for reproduction by building it into the cabinet.

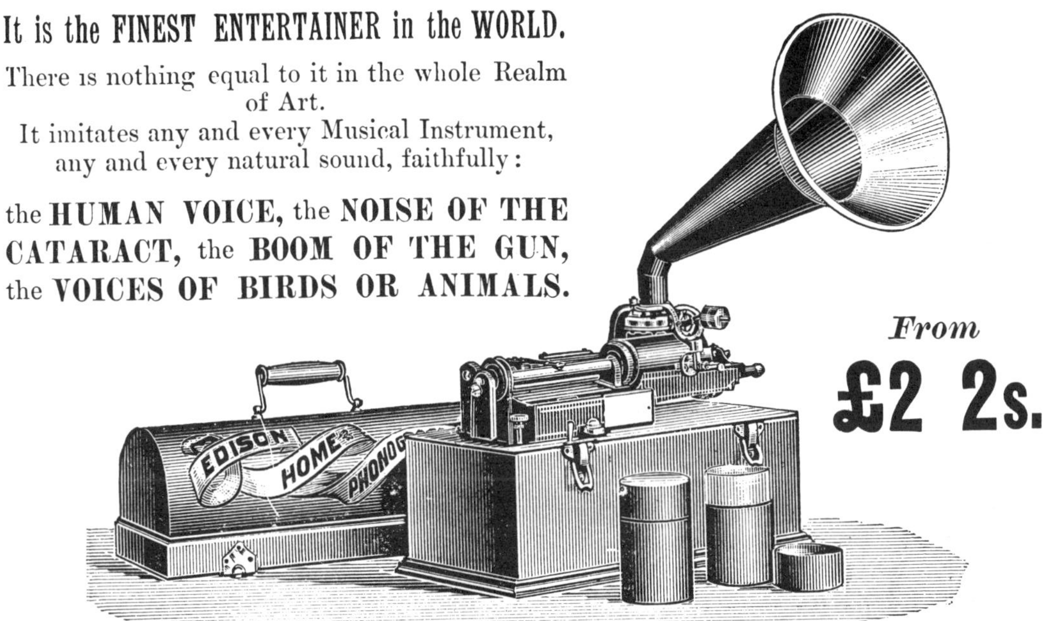

An 1899 advertisement for a phonograph, or gramophone.

An Edwardian family admires
a new gramophone.

Records were made harder, sound reproduced better and there was a longer playing time. The industry went well until the beginning of radio broadcasting in the 1920s, when many companies went bankrupt.

During all this time another industry—the cinema—had been growing up. Thomas Edison had a hand in this, too. When he first invented his phonograph he toyed with the idea of supplementing the sound with pictures. He began thinking about the problems of motion-picture photography when his phonograph was nearly finished. He had been inspired by photo-

graphers who had succeeded in taking somewhat crude
motion pictures and had invented projectors for them,
although none proved practicable. On 14th April 1894
he emerged from his laboratory with the first motion
picture. He called his invention the *Kinetoscope*. The
film showed a sneeze; it lasted for 15 seconds and was
viewed through a peephole.

The Kinetoscope was so popular that it was copied
all over Europe. But the number who could watch the
film at one time was limited. What was needed was an
instrument that would project the image on to a screen
so that a lot of people could see the film together.

The following year various projectors were developed using some of the Kinetoscope features. Edison,
realizing that the novelty of the peephole Kinetoscope
would fade, turned his mind to producing a projector.
The public presentation of what he claimed was his

Edison's travelling moving-
picture show comes to town,
1904.

projector, the Vitascope, took place at Koster and Bial's music hall in New York in 1896.

This was the beginning of the motion picture as a form of popular entertainment. Within six months Edison had sold 80 of his projectors. The first films were only 50 feet long and lasted less than a minute. Edison built a battery-driven camera, the kinetograph, the size of an upright piano. To house it he built the first cinema—called the Black Maria—a small tar-paper-covered studio near his laboratory at West Orange, New Jersey.

Film shows consisted of about a dozen short films on one reel, many of which came from the old peepshows. Then the public lost interest, and producers were forced to think of something new. Richard Hollaman, of the Eden Musée in New York, made the first attempt to tell a story. He produced a long film of the Ober-ammergau Passion Play. It was not a genuine repro-

A still from one of the earliest films, *The Train Arrives at the Station,* made in France in 1895.

duction of the real spectacle as advertised, but had been made on the roof of the Grand Central Palace. The public was so impressed that it did not complain when it discovered it had been fooled.

By 1900 more films were telling stories. A turning point came in 1903 when Edwin Porter produced *The Great Train Robbery* with Marie Murray as leading lady. A long series of similar films followed, and with them the growth of the nickelodeon or five-cent theatre to show the films.

For the first quarter of the twentieth century the motion-picture industry prospered. Equipment and films became more costly and complicated, but basically nothing changed. They were still silent films, with subtitles to convey subtle action and dialogue. Ever-present in the minds of inventors was the idea of linking

Hollywood in its early days. On the left a new studio is being built.

sound with the images, quite the opposite of Edison's original idea to link images with sound. The obvious choice for this link-up was the phonograph. Leon Gaumont in France had produced some short sound films, using the idea of synchronizing a moving picture with a phonograph record. Many other crazy and ingenious schemes were devised to overcome this problem of synchronization. One inventor linked a phonograph to his projector motor with a system of belts and pulleys which ran the whole length of the house from booth to screen.

By 1912 enough interest had been shown to prompt Edison to make some talking pictures. But while all this was going on, Eugene Lauste in England had made and patented the basic method for recording sound on film.

Picture theatres were growing bigger, and this increased the problems of amplification and synchronization. Lauste's equipment and the phonograph were not loud enough for a large auditorium. The problem was solved by the audion amplifier, a selenium vacuum tube, developed by Lee de Forest just before the First World War, which was used during the war for long-distance radio and telephone communications because it could increase volume. The Bell Telephone Company was assigned the patents, but after the war de Forest concentrated on talking pictures.

He thought the idea of using a phonograph was ridiculous; synchronization would be ruined if either the film or the record was damaged. So he turned his attention to recording sound directly on to film. The way to do this, he discovered, was to transform sound waves into electricity that could be photographed in black and white on a strip of celluloid. The film, when passed under a photoelectric cell in the projector, would change the images back to sound.

In 1923 de Forest was showing his phonofilms at theatres, but they caused little excitement. Meanwhile scientists at the Bell Telephone laboratories were

Above: A still from one of the most famous films ever made, the
Russian *Battleship Potemkin,* made in the 1920's. *Below:* A scene
from *The Jazz Singer,* the film which made "talkies" popular.

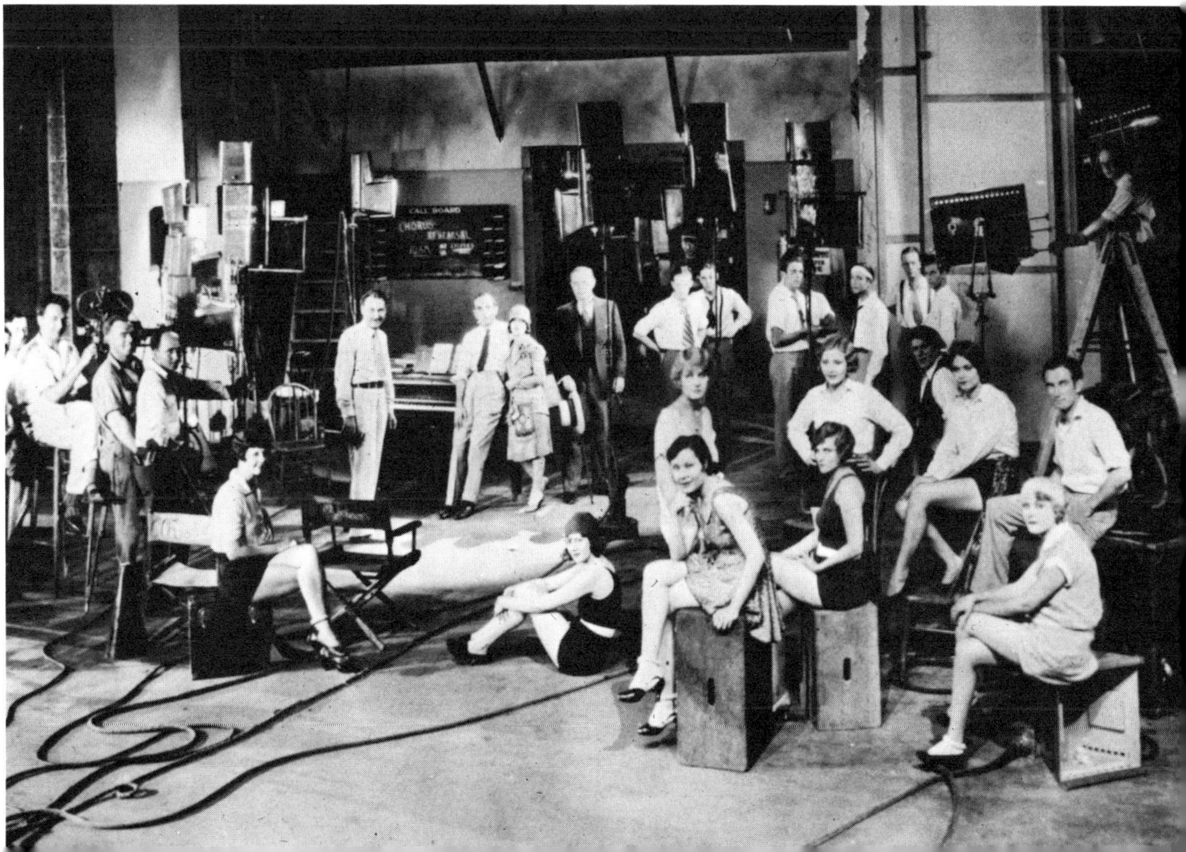

trying to combine the phonograph and the motion picture. By 1926 they had produced a special turntable synchronized to the projection motors which could hold discs large enough to last the length of a film. Warner Brothers, who were near to bankruptcy, seized this opportunity and introduced the Vitaphone in August of that year in a programme of several talking and musical shorts, featuring John Barrymore in *Don Juan*. Again, it caused no great stir. The break came in October the next year with the presentation of Al Jolson in *The Jazz Singer*. The public was delighted. By 1930 silent films were dead. Warner Brothers eventually gave up sound-on-disc films completely.

The idea of colour motion pictures had always attracted producers. During the first years of the twentieth century, films were coloured by hand. Rows of girls, each one with her own colour, would follow the images from frame to frame. Then in 1905 Pathé introduced a semi-automatic stencil system that lasted until 1930. Meanwhile a two-colour process, Kinemacolour, had been invented in England by Charles Urban and G. Albert Smith. The process passed alternate red and green filters in front of the lens at the time of photography and again at the time of projection.

Audiences were attracted by colour films but they also derived a great deal of amusement from them. The two-colour process looked false, and the colour followed a moving object rather than being part of it. The colour of a man's trousers would be walking behind him.

Technicolor was the answer. It was started in 1915 by Herbert Kalmus and a team of physicists from the Massachusetts Institute of Technology. They used a prism to split up the light beam into two as it entered the camera, one beam being at the red–orange end of the spectrum and the other at the blue–green end. When developed the film was passed through dyes to achieve its natural colour. Demand was so high for

these films that laboratories could not keep pace;
films were done so quickly they were often fuzzy or
blurred. And so audiences declined. The announcement
of a three-colour process was not enough to interest
them. It was not until the success of *Gone With The Wind*
that colour films were firmly established in the public's
favour.

The first regular television programme was broadcast
by the B.B.C. on 2nd November 1936 after many
years of research. In 1923 J. L. Baird in England and
C. F. Jenkins in America transmitted crude black and
white silhouettes in motion. Two years later they
succeeded in transmitting moving pictures. This was
the start of television; but the pictures were so crude
that a great deal of work had yet to be done.

Baird in London with his new
television transmitter.

We owe our modern television systems to a Russian, Boris Rosing, and an Englishman, A. A. Campbell-Swinton, who in 1907, independent of each other, suggested using cathode rays for reproducing the image. A cathode-ray tube had already been made in 1897 by K. F. Braun.

By the end of 1948 television was free of wartime restrictions and evolved rapidly. Colour television was introduced in 1954, after 50 years of research.

In the record industry stereophonic sound had been introduced. The Bell Telephone Company was the first to demonstrate the effect of stereo reproduction when the sound of an orchestra playing in Philadelphia was heard over loud-speakers in Washington. The sound was transmitted directly over telephone lines. Columbia and R.C.A. introduced fine-groove records, and by the 1950's the stereo system was ready for everyday use, two separate microphones being used in recording and two separate loudspeakers in reproduction.

Tape recording has come a long way since the early days of piano wire. We can now buy small cassette players and cassette tapes which are much lighter than records to carry around. It is possible that cassettes will take over completely from records in the next decade, especially as they too now offer stereo reproduction.

The cinema had to make many improvements to compete with television. Cinerama was introduced in 1952. This had a wide curving screen picture that was composed of three separate film strips with seven-channel stereo sound equipment. It was popular at the time but it never pulled back the huge audiences of the 1930's into the cinemas.

Television is now widely used in education. Lectures and demonstrations on specialist subjects are regularly broadcast to schools. Many teaching hospitals use closed-circuit television to let students watch an experienced surgeon's hands performing a delicate operation, a method that overcomes the problems of infection and of overcrowding in the operating theatre.

Industry, too, has come to rely on television a great deal. Cameras can transmit at close range things happening at critical points in a chemical process at which an operator could not be present, for example when television is used to show the remote handling of radio-active material.

It can be used under the sea; where a human diver can only go down a few hundred feet, the camera can go down to the sea bed. The camera can take biological pictures and can help in the search for sunken ships. In space television is all-important. Do you remember watching the Moon landings on T.V.?

Films are used in schools; today few schools are without a projector. Records are used in literature and music lessons. Many famous actors and actresses have recorded plays or excerpts from books for this purpose. Tape recorders have been shown to be a great help in teaching a foreign language.

So what began as entertainment is now also part of our educational system. Thomas Edison knew this all along. When he invented the phonograph he prophesied that one day it would replace books completely.

The first men on the Moon.
People all over the world
watched this event, as it
happened, on television, and
President Nixon broadcast a
message to the Moon.

11 : Today and Tomorrow

The application of technology to printing continued through the twentieth century. These advances contributed to the increase in circulation of the popular press in the first half of the century. The *Daily Mail*, whose circulation had reached the 1 million mark during the Boer War (1899–1902), achieved 1¼ million in the 1920's. The *Daily Express* and a Sunday newspaper, the *People*, were equally successful. In the early 1960's the *Daily Express* had reached 4½ million but was later overtaken by the tabloid *Daily Mirror* that had a vast working class readership. The *News of the World* on Sundays reached a never-before all-time high of 7 million. Actual readership was even higher.

Today the influence of the national press, judged by copies sold, is slowly declining. Circulations have fallen. In early 1973 the *Daily Express* stood at 3,289,188; the *Daily Mirror* at 4,227,563; the *Daily Mail* at 1,683,945; the *People* at 4,422,902; the *News of the World* at 5,939,821.

This is partly because of the growth of radio and television. But another factor is the changing status of the newspaper owner. In the eighteenth and nineteenth centuries proprietors tended to be editors, and newspapers were viewed with deep suspicion by governments. Many journalists had been to prison for breaking anti-press laws. The present century has seen the growth of press empires, with several newspapers under a

Checking a new communications satellite before launching. It is jointly owned by more than 60 nations, and is now in orbit sending all kinds of messages from one side of the world to the other.

single ownership. Politicians and businessmen began to appreciate the influence of the press, and to cultivate newspaper proprietors, who in turn valued the prestige and political and social influence of their position. Most of the heads of the newspaper empires were offered and accepted peerages, a thing impossible to imagine happening to John Wilkes or William Cobbett. The proprietors became part of the Establishment; journalism became respectable.

Today there is less inclination for the press to attack injustice and to expose corruption in the Establishment or linked with it. There are exceptions, notably the *Sunday Times, Observer, Times* and *Guardian*, but they are getting fewer. In America the work of the *Washington Post* in investigating and exposing the Watergate scandal is praiseworthy. But in the main the traditional role of newspapers to investigate and expose matters of public importance is being taken over increasingly by "fringe" publications such as *Private Eye, Time Out* and *Socialist Worker*. These often publish news items that have been submitted by journalists to the national press and not used by them. It is these fringe publications

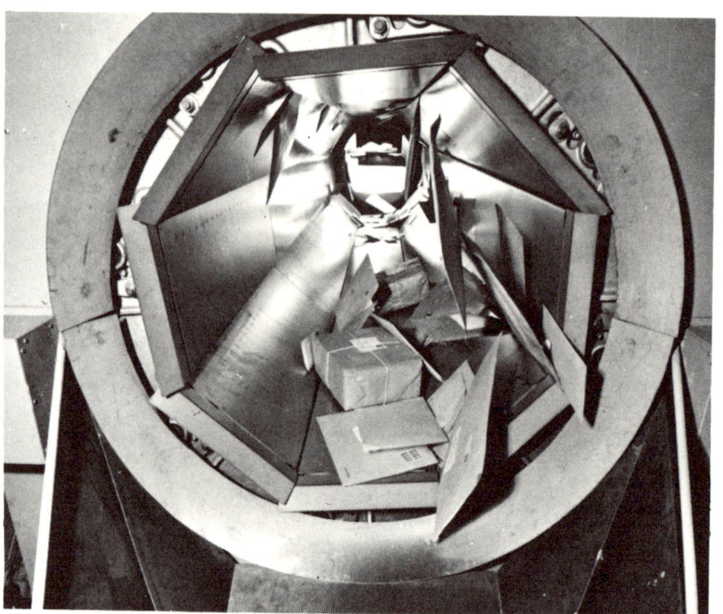

A modern Post Office segregating machine sorts letters into different shapes and sizes.

that follow the traditions of the early British press, and the antagonism they generate is like that experienced by Wilkes, Cobbett, Walter and W. T. Stead. Inevitably, as fringe journals lack the resources to check every story, they make some mistakes and are prosecuted for libel.

Cheaper methods of printing have made the public less dependent on well-established newspapers and magazines. Improved xerox copying and offset printing techniques have resulted in many new periodicals appearing, with small circulations or production runs. Thus unfashionable opinions and new ideas get a hearing, diversity is catered for, and there is the opportunity for editors who recognize developments in popular taste to exploit them—as has been shown by the rapid growth of *Private Eye* and *Time Out*.

Newspapers, as huge business enterprises, now need to attract advertising to create profits for shareholders. This has led to intense competition between them. Since sensationalism has been shown to improve sales, much unwarranted sensationalism has resulted. The Radcliffe Tribunal of 1962, investigating the arrest of a spy in the Admiralty, referred in its report of 1963 to the stories in the press of the inefficiency of Government ministers and civil servants. At least 250 of these stories published in the popular press, in particular in the *Daily Express, Daily Mirror, Daily Mail* and the *People*, were untrue, and some of them were complete fabrications written without a shred of evidence. Confidence in the national press was shaken.

Yet investigation, revelation and the provision of background information is what the press does best. Radio and television have now taken the lead as providers of instant news. Britain now has seven BBC and five IBA television stations, plus four BBC country-wide radio stations and eleven local ones. At least the same number of commercial local radio stations are planned. We use four international satellites (with four in reserve for back-up in case of breakdown) to get instant news from all over the world. This news comes so fast and furious that people cannot assess its importance. Newspapers can provide these assessments.

In Britain neither radio nor television is prepared to mount a continuous campaign against injustice or corruption. Its controllers seem afraid of influencing public opinion—a very popular broadcaster of foreign affairs, Vernon Bartlett, was dropped in the early 1930s because of his growing influence on public opinion towards views which often ran counter to government policy. Under the present set-up, radio and television will remain channels of semi-official communication. In commercial radio and television, dependent for profits on advertising, a debasement similar to that seen in the popular press is apparent, with the majority of programmes mediocre in content.

But developments in the field of electronic video recording make it likely that the news content of television will be separated from the entertainment. Experts have forecast that in the future every individual will have his own television newspaper. Television "consumers" will have their interests computerized. All the media will be scanned for items to match against these interests, and the material will be relayed to him through his television set.

There will be more use of radio and television in the education of both children and adults. The role they play in schools has already been demonstrated. For adults in the future they will be an essential way of finding out about new developments in science and technology. An American expert says: "At the rate at which knowledge is growing, by the time the child born today graduates from college, the amount of knowledge in the world will be four times as great. By the time that same child is 50 years old, it will be thirty-two times as great, and 97 per cent of everything known in the world will have been learned since the time he was born." The role of communications, of sending messages, in the life of man will increase as his store of knowledge grows.

Date Chart

B.C.

Stone Age	Pictures of animals carved by man on cave walls.
About 3000	Sumerians in Mesopotamia (Iraq) use picture writing in which the picture represents a sound in spoken language. Egyptians have pigeon-messenger service.
About 2400	Egyptians make paper from papyrus, and ink from charcoal.
About 2300	Egyptians introduce human messenger service.
About 1000	Phoenicians perfect picture alphabet of 22 sounds.
About 950	King Solomon and the Queen of Sheba exchange messages by carrier pigeon.
529	Cyrus the Great, Emperor of Persia, establishes messenger service throughout Persian Empire, using relay system of postriders.
490	Pheidippides the Messenger brings news of the Battle of Marathon to the Athenians. Persians at the Battle of Marathon practise heliograph signalling by means of Sun's reflection on burnished shields.
About 100	Romans develop alphabet in use today throughout the western world. Romans established post house system for messengers. Romans use stylus for writing on clay tablets.

A.D.

About 200	Chinese manufacture paper from bamboo, silk or linen.
778	The *Chanson de Roland* tells of Roland's horn-blowing feat before his death fighting the Saracens.
About 800	Chinese invent printing by blocks, one for each page.
868	Wooden blocks used by the Chinese in the printing of the book "roll" (16 feet long) of the *Diamond Sutra*, a Buddhist scripture.
About 1000	Movable type clay blocks perfected by Chinese, one for each letter or ideograph.
1100	Henry I of England establishes King's Messenger Service.
About 1400	Graphite used for writing.
1440	Johann Gutenberg in Germany experiments with printing techniques that form basis of modern printing industry. Makes moulds for casting metal type, enabling individual letters to be used repeatedly.
1456	Two-volume Gutenberg Bible printed in Germany.
1474	At Bruges, William Caxton prints first book in English language.
1477	William Caxton produces first book printed in English in England.
1570	Ensigns of standard design used by English ships as means of identification.

1588	English warned of the approach of the Spanish Armada by lighting of beacon fires across the country.
1621	First pamphlets printed in England.
1649	Oliver Cromwell censors the English press.
1650	Otto von Guericke produces electric charge in a ball of sulphur.
1657	First Postmaster General appointed in England.
1663	In England Licensing Act seeks to control press through system of licences.
1680	Penny Post introduced into London area by private enterprise.
1690	William Rittenhouse builds first paper mill in Pennsylvania, America, using rag to make paper. In England *Worcester Post*, first provincial newspaper, appears.
1711	Government imposes Stamp Duty in England on newspapers in attempt to reduce the influence of the press.
1720	René de Réamur makes paper from wood.
1753	Benjamin Franklin appointed Postmaster of the American colonies. Chain of post stations established between Maine and Georgia.
1775	Paul Revere warns American colonists of movements of British troops; War of American Independence starts.
1784	In Britain, Royal Mail coaches on the London to Bath run cover 106 miles in 16 hours.
1790	In France, Claude Chappé demonstrates optical telegraph.
1791	The *Observer* commences publication in London.
1793–4	In France, construction starts on optical telegraph relay stations over 40 miles, and Chappé's invention comes into public service.
1795	Lord George Murray's optical telegraph in use in Britain.
1800	Printing presses made of iron come into use.
1814	Steam-operated printing press installed by *The Times*.
1815	Battle of Waterloo; Scots Greys ignore bugle signal to break off engagement and are decimated by French.
1817	International code of signalling for ships adopted by maritime nations in western world.
1819	Pens with steel nibs made in Britain by Samuel Harrison.
1821	First publication of *Manchester Guardian* (later the *Guardian*), famous British provincial daily paper.
1822	First publication of *Sunday Times*, famous British Sunday paper.
1827	SS *Curaçao* of Holland makes first steam-powered crossing of the Atlantic. In Britain Tally Ho stage coach service from London to Birmingham covers 109 miles at over 14 m.p.h.
1830	Railways used in Britain to transport mail. Daguerre, French painter, begins to develop a camera for taking pictures.
1835	Von Schilling demonstrates 5-needle electro-magnetic telegraph in Bonn.
1835	James Clerk Maxwell, Scottish physicist, publishes electromagnetic theory of light. Growth of turnpike companies in Britain, each responsible for upkeep of short stretch of road.
1837	Cooke and Wheatstone demonstrate 5-needle electro-magnetic telegraph in London. First telegraph line laid by the London and North Western Railway between Euston and Camden to make use of the Cooke and Wheatstone invention. Samuel Morse demonstrates Morse electro-magnetic signalling system in New York.

1838	SS *Great Western* crosses the Atlantic in 15 days.
1839	World's first public telegraph office opens in London.
1840	Penny Post introduced in Britain.
1843	*News of the World* published, first popular Sunday newspaper with mass appeal.
1844	Samuel Morse sends first commercial message by electro-magnetic telegraph line from Baltimore to Washington.
1853	Undersea cable laid between France and Britain.
1854	Undersea cable laid between Ireland and Britain.
1855	In Britain *Daily Telegraph* commences publication.
1857	Leon Scott builds first machine to record sound.
1858	Cyrus W. Field and fellow engineers lay undersea cable between America and Europe. Breaks after 2 months.
1860	Pony Express postal service starts in America.
1861	Telegraph wires connect New York with San Francisco.
1862	SS *Scotia* crosses Atlantic in 9 days.
1863	Rotary press invented for newspaper production.
	Red Flag Act passed in Britain restricting speed of steam coaches to 2 m.p.h. in towns and 4 m.p.h. in the country.
1865–6	S.S. *Great Eastern* used to lay cable undersea between America and Europe.
1866	Heliograph system, using sun's rays on mirrors, brought into operation by British in India with great success. Messages exchanged over 100 miles along line of hill stations.
1867	Punched tape used for electro-magnetic telegraph.
1868	In America Christopher L. Sholes produces first satisfactory typewriter.
1870	Berne Conference. International agreement reached on postal services.
	Siege of Paris; pigeon post sole method of communication with outside world.
1876	Alexander Graham Bell patents invention of telephone.
1878	Bell visits London, links Parliament with Fleet Street with telephone system.
1883	Parcel post service introduced into Britain.
1884	Lewis Edson Waterman patents first fountain pen in New York.
1885	Ottmar Mergenthaler in America invents the linotype machine which speeds up printing process.
1887	Thomas Edison invents phonograph.
1889	George Eastman produces lightweight camera and roll film.
1894	Cheap gramophone record discs made by Berliner Gramophone Company.
	Edison Kinetoscope, first motion picture apparatus.
1895	In Britain, Lord Rutherford transmits radio waves over $\frac{3}{4}$ mile.
	Guglielmo Marconi transmits radio waves in Italy.
	New York Journal, the first "sensational" newspaper is published.
1896	In Britain the *Daily Mail*, first daily newspaper with a mass circulation is launched.
	Edison invents Vitascope, forerunner of the motion picture camera.
	Marconi sends Morse code radio signals 2 miles.
1901	Marconi's wireless transmitting station at Poldhu, Cornwall, sends signal across the Atlantic.
1903	*The Great Train Robbery*, first commercial motion picture.
1906	Professor Ambrose Fleming invents audion electric tube.
1912	SS *Titanic* sinks on maiden voyage.
	In Britain the State takes over private telephone companies.
	In America the world's first scheduled air flight operates from New York to Washington.
1919	In Europe, scheduled air flights used for mail deliveries.

1920	In Pittsburgh, U.S.A., first public radio transmission station opens.
1922	In Britain, first public radio station opens at Savoy Hill, London.
1926	Sound films shown to general public.
1934	Mail air service established between Inverness and Orkneys.
1938	SS *Queen Mary*, Britain, gains record for fastest crossing of the Atlantic in 3 days 21 hours 42 minutes.
1940	Television made available to the public in Britain. Tape recorders perfected.
1941	In Britain, communist daily newspaper *Daily Worker* suppressed by Government. Ban lifted in 1942 after Hitler attacks U.S.S.R.
About 1950	V.H.F. introduced and use of short waves in radio and television improves reception.
1952	SS *United States*, America, gains record for fastest crossing of the Atlantic in 3 days 10 hours 40 minutes.
1954	First colour television.
1956	Undersea telephone cable links America with Europe.
1957	U.S.S.R. rocket launches satellite into Space. Satellite circles Earth at 17,000 m.p.h.
1958	S.T.D. telephone dialling system introduced to Britain. Queen Elizabeth II dials first trunk call—Bristol to Edinburgh.
1961	U.S.S.R. sends first man, Yuri Gagarin, into Space.
1962	Telstar I, communications satellite, placed in orbit by U.S.A. Events in Europe seen by viewers in America at the moment of happening, and *vice versa*.
1963	International Subscriber Dialling is extended in Britain, allowing general public to dial calls to the rest of Europe.
1965	Early Bird, first commercial communications satellite launched by the U.S.A., hovers 22,300 miles over the Atlantic and relays messages between North America and Europe. U.S.S.R. launches communications satellite Molniya I.

Picture Credits

Glossary

AUDION AMPLIFIER, or SELENIUM VACUUM TUBE. Early type of valve for amplifying a stream of electrons.

CASSETTE. Holder of reel of magnetic tape that fits into tape deck of recorder.

CATHODE RAY. Stream of electrons emitted from surface of cathode (negative terminal of electric cell) that can be redirected towards an applied magnetic field.

ELECTRO-MAGNETISM. Magnetism produced by an electric current.

ELECTRO-MAGNETIC THEORY OF LIGHT. The theory which accounts for the phenomena of radio transmission and of light in terms of electro-magnetic waves.

EDISON'S VARIABLE CONTACT CARBON TRANSMITTER. An early form of transmitter that through electrical energy sent acoustic information over a distance along wires.

ELECTRONIC VIDEO. Television signals sent by electron beam.

FRANKING MARK. A mark on mail to allow it to go through the post without a stamp being affixed.

GRAMOPHONE. An instrument for reproducing sound using a stylus in contact with a spiral groove on a revolving disc.

MORSE CODE. Various combinations of dots and dashes that comprise a signalling system perfected by Samuel Morse for use on a telegraphic circuit, and later used in radio transmission.

MORSE BUZZER. A device used in the sending of messages in Morse code, that opens and closes contacts in the circuit to modulate the electric current.

PICTOGRAPH. A series of pictures, each representing a sound, drawn on clay with a stylus, in use about 3000 B.C. and subsequently as a means of communication.

PHONOGRAPH. Early name for gramophone (see Gramophone).

PHONAUTOGRAPH. Term not now in use describing an instrument that records sound automatically.

PHOTOCONDUCTIVE CAMERA. One in which the optical image is focussed on to a surface, the electrical resistance of the surface being controlled by illumination. Used in television.

RADIO BEACON. Stationary radio transmitter which transmits steady beams of radiation in specified direction for the guidance of ships and aircraft with radio direction finders.

SATELLITES. A vehicle put into orbit around the Earth or other planet and used to transmit information by means of radio waves, using antennae for reception and transmission.

STEREOPHONIC SOUND. Sound produced by a system which gives the hearer the impression that the sound is coming from two or more directions.

TELEGRAPH. From two Greek words meaning "writing from a distance." Originally used by the Greeks to describe a system of communicating by flags, torches or other visual indicators. The letters making up a message were represented by agreed signals. Brought into use again by Claude Chappé in 1790 who used jointed bars to produce the visual signals, and today used to describe messages sent by Morse code along wires.

TELEPHONE. Apparatus for transmitting speech over a distance by audiofrequency current sent along wires. In long-distance communication by telephone valve amplifiers are used (known as repeaters) to

make up for the loss of power due to the distance
the current travels.

THERMIONIC VALVE. One containing heated cathode(s)
from which electrons are emitted. Its invention
revolutionised radio and telecommunications.

TRANSMITTING STATION. The terminal point at which
radio waves are generated, their frequency modified
and transmission carried out by means of an antenna.

For Further Reading

Agnes Allen, *The Story of the Book* (Faber, 1952).

Catherine Baker, *Talking about the Media* (Wayland,
1973).

Philip Bono and Kenneth Gatland, *Frontiers of Space*
(Blandford, 1969).

Asa Briggs, *The Birth of Broadcasting* (Oxford University
Press, 1961).

E. H. Jolly, *Telecommunications* (Weidenfeld & Nicolson,
1961).

Egon Larsen, *Transport* (Phoenix House, 1959).

Harry Edward Neal, *Communication from Stone Age to
Space Age* (Phoenix House, 1963).

Alan Pitt Robins, *Newspapers Today* (Oxford University Press, 1956).

Frank Staff, *The Penny Post* (Lutterworth, 1964).

Francis Williams, *The Right to Know: The Rise of the
World's Press* (Longmans 1969)

Raymond Williams, *Communications* (Chatto & Windus,
1969).

Index

Advertising, 68–9, 119, 120
Airships, 50–1
Ampère, André Marie, 75, 78
Audion vacuum tube, 99

Baird, J. L., 111
B.B.C., 99–100, 111, 119
Beacons, fire 15–16, 19, 27
—radio 95, 119
Bell, Alexander Graham 73, 86–90, 101
Bell Telephone Company, 87, 108, 112
Bells, 19
Berliner, Emile, 102
Bugle calls, 14, 19
Bullock, William, 73–4

Cables, undersea, 82, 89
Call posts, 10
Campbell-Swinton, A. A. 112
Caxton, William, 56
Chanson de Roland, 12, 14
Chappé, Claude, 20–1
Cinema, 105–113
Clay tablets, 31
Clippers, 46
Coaches, 39–41
Coffee houses, 63
Cooke, William Fothergill, 76, 82
Curaçao, SS, 45

Daily Express, 73, 116, 119
Daily Mail, 72, 73, 116, 119
Daily Mirror, 73, 116, 119
Daily Telegraph, 72
Daily Universal Register, 66
De Forest, Lee, 99, 108
Drums, 10, 11, 12, 18, 19

Edison, Thomas, 101–5, 113
Electric Telegraph Company, 77
Electro-magnetism, 75, 78, 92–3

Flags, 20, 22
Fringe publications, 118, 119

Gaumont, Louis, 108
Gramophone, 102–4
Great Britain, SS, 45
Great Western, SS, 45
Guardian, 69, 118
Gutenberg Bible, 55

Harmsworth, Alfred and Harold, 72
Henry, Joseph, 75, 79
Hertz, Heinrich, 92–3
Hill, Rowland, 43–44, 51
Horn, 12, 14, 19

International Code, 22

Jazz Singer, The, 110
Jensen, Nicholas, 56

Kinetoscope, 105

Letter boxes, 43
Letters, 25, 32–47, 6.
Lighthouses, 17
Lucana, SS, 46

Mail coaches, 39, 41, 48
Marconi, Guglieme, 93–6, 98
Marconi Wireless Telegraphy Company, 94, 95
Mass meetings, 66
Maxwell, James Clerk, 92
Mergenthaler, Ottmar, 74
Messages, 19–20, 26
Messenger service, 27, 29, 30, 31, 32, 36
Mirrors, 17–18
Morse, Samuel, 75, 78–9, 82
Morse Code, 22–3, 79–83
Murray, Lord George, 21

News of the World, 72, 116
Newspapers, 59–74, 113, 116–7
Newspaper Stamp Act, 63

Observer, 72, 118
Odeon Company, 102
Oersted, H. C., 75
Oriental, SS, 46

Packet boats, 44
Page, Dr C. G., 73
Papyrus, 32
People, 116, 117
Pharos of Alexandria, 17
Pheidippides, 27
Phonograph, 102, 113
Pigeon post, 23, 24, 29
Poetry, 27
Pony Express, 50
Post bags, 33
Post houses, 32
Post, parcel, 49

Post, penny, 38, 43–4
Postal charges, 37, 42–4
Postal service, 32–3, 35–7, 47–53
Post Office, The, 38, 89
Post Office, Travelling, 48
Post Office vans, 49
Press, freedom of. 65–66
Printing, 53–62
Private Eye, 118, 119

Queen Mary, SS, 46

Radio, 91–3, 97–9, 119
Railways, 41, 47–9, 76–7
Reuter, Julius, 73, 84–5
Revere, Paul, 27–9
Roads, Roman, 33, 39
—Turnpike, 40
Rothschild, Nathan, 23
Rutherford, Ernest, 93

Satellites, 119–120
Schilling, Baron von, 75
Scott, C. P., 69
Signals, prearranged, 19
—smoke, 19
Sirius, SS, 45
Stamps, 44
Stamp Act, 63–4
Sunday Times, 72, 118

Tape recording, 112
Telegraph, 20, 51, 73, 78, 81–4, 86
—optical, 20
Telephone, 51, 73, 86–9
Teleprinter, 51
Television, 111–3, 119–120
Telex, 51
Time Out, 118, 119
Times, The, 66, 68, 69, 72, 118
Titanic, SS, 97–8

United States, SS, 46

Walter, John, 68
Walter, John junior, 68
Warner Brothers, 110
Washington Post, 118
Weekly Register, 68
Wells Fargo, 50
Wheatstone, Sir Charles, 73, 76, 82–3
Whistling, 18
Wilkes, John, 65–6
Writing, 31–2